Love—how many times during a day
do we hear the word?
But what does it mean to love?

John was a very old man when he wrote
his poignant letters of love, light and life.
He had experienced the tumultuous half-century
during which the Christian church
was born and took root.
He had seen all of Jesus' apostles die,
many by martyrdom,
and was the last to survive.
He had lived under persecution.

John knew what love really was.
This man whom Jesus
called the "son of thunder"
was also the "beloved apostle"
and became the tender and loving patriarch
to his "little children."

It behooves every Christian living
in these times, so very similar to those
during which the apostle
wrote 1, 2, and 3 John,
to discover and experience the love John knew.

LETTERS TO CHILDREN OF LIGHT

COMMENTARY ON FIRST, SECOND & THIRD JOHN

E.M. Blaiklock

A BIBLE
COMMENTARY
FOR LAYMEN

Regal Books A Division of G/L Publications
Ventura, California, U.S.A.

Other good reading in this series:
Loved and Forgiven (Colossians)
    by Lloyd John Ogilvie
Pass It On (1 & 2 Timothy)
    by Robert Mounce
Patterns for Power (Parables of Luke)
    by Stuart Briscoe

A Gospel Light Teacher's Manual and Student Discovery Guide for Bible study groups using *Letters to Children of Light* are available from your church supplier.

The foreign language publishing of all Regal books is under the direction of GLINT. GLINT provides financial and technical help for the adaptation, translation and publishing of books in more than 85 languages for millions of people worldwide.

For more information write: GLINT, P.O. Box 6688, Ventura, CA 93006.

The Scripture quotations in *Letters to Children of Light* are from the *New American Standard Bible*. © The Lockman Foundation 1960, 1962, 1963, 1968, 1971, 1972, 1973, 1975. Used by permission.
Also from the *Authorized King James Version (KJV)*.
Phillips, THE NEW TESTAMENT IN MODERN ENGLISH, Revised Edition, J.B. Phillips, Translator. © J.B. Phillips 1958, 1960, 1972. Used by permission of Macmillan Publishing Co., Inc.
The translation used for the text discussion is that of the author, E.M. Blaiklock.

Sixth Printing, 1981

Published by Regal Books
A Division of G/L Publications
Ventura, California 93006
Printed in U.S.A.

Library of Congress Catalog Card No. 75-14883
ISBN 0-8307-0460-4

CONTENTS

INTRODUCTION

Understanding a literary document means studying the circumstances in which it was written, knowing something of the author and knowing those to whom its message was addressed. The books of the Bible are no exception and we shall try to apply this to John's letters. We shall look briefly at the Church as it was in the closing years of the first century, we shall meet John in his extreme and mellow age, and we shall catch a glimpse of his congregation and the wider public to whom his words were addressed.

In studying the First Epistle of John it must be borne continually in mind that the letter was probably written to accompany the Gospel of John. The New Testament was approaching completion. The three synoptic Gospels were in circulation; the writings of Luke were generally known; the letters of Paul, Peter, Jude and James were in cherished possession of the Church. With the ministry of Paul behind, with half a century of Christian experience to shape the life and sharpen the problems of the

Christian community, with the somber shadow of persecution a fact of Christian life, and with a half-century of pondering over those three years in Palestine to enrich his memory, John felt the urge to write his Gospel. That precious book was to close the New Testament. It was to show Christ afresh against the background of the years and in relation to the now completed body of Christian truth.

The letter dealt more directly with the spiritual problems of the hour and attacked error with a directness which would have been out of place in the Gospel of John. The letter applied the truth developed in the Gospel. It formed a sermon upon it. The letter, together with the Gospel, cast the only light we have upon the last thirty years of the first century. That is why it is important to look around and behind the words as well as into them.

We find more than history there. We find the author. And to gain some notion of the mind of one who walked with Christ, half a century beyond those momentous days, is fascinatingly interesting. We know little of the apostle's life over those fifty years, but enough perhaps to follow its main outlines. Several references in Acts and one in Galatians suggest that he remained in Jerusalem until about A.D. 50. It is possible that he was in Rome at the time of Nero's cruel persecution in the middle sixties and probable that, after the martyrdom of Peter and Paul, he went to Ephesus. His mature ministry was certainly exercised here. The "seven churches of Revelation" were no doubt his "circuit." Revelation itself was written during this period.

The letter, like others in the New Testament, was written in deep disturbance of spirit and in ardent desire to defend the faith. Dangerous heresies were abroad. It is important to understand the difficulties of the early Church and the dangers which beset its path. We speak with considerable looseness of "the early Church." One commentator remarks that getting back to the life of the early Church is simply to talk of what we do not understand. Paul struggled and prayed to get it away from its own feeble life, to lift it to a higher level of truth and strength.

Most of Paul's writings are the documents of that conflict. The same is true of the letters of John. We understand them better if we bear the problem in mind.

When John wrote his first letter from Ephesus, Jerusalem had fallen and the pride of Judaism lay broken. The old struggle to debase the Christian faith and transform it into a sect of Judaism had failed. But the attempt to work out a compromise with paganism, and to interpret the new faith as a liberal philosophy was at its height. That is why John's epistles are so vitally interesting today. They are the first answer of the true tradition to liberalism. The battle was within, the battle which Paul had foreseen in his farewell address to the Ephesian elders thirty or more years earlier (Acts 20:29,30).

Irenaeus, who lived from about A.D. 130 to the end of the second century, remarked of the Fourth Gospel that "John, the disciple of the Lord, desired by the declaration of his Gospel to remove the error which had been sown among men by Cerinthus, and much earlier by those who are called Nicolaitans." The same purpose applies to the Epistle.

Who were these sectaries? Cerinthus appears to have been a forerunner to those who, in the second century, were called Gnostics. Their doctrine was a species of

8

theosophy. The deep things of the gospel were for the enlightened few, for those who knew, for that is what the word Gnostic means. They were a sort of self-constituted spiritual élite, exempt from the rules of holy conduct which were observed by the simple souls who took the gospel to mean what it said. Cerinthus, clearly of their ancestry, had some special notions about the nature of Christ. He distinguished Christ from Jesus. Jesus was the human son of Joseph and Mary into whom the Christ came at the Baptism only to withdraw before the Crucifixion. It was Jesus who died, not Christ. John clearly has this pernicious error in mind in the first chapters of the letter. It is curious to see the same ancient error rise again with odd distinctions drawn between the Jesus of history and the Christ of faith.

And the Nicolaitans? It is clear to any careful reader of the New Testament that there was a group in the Church whose trail begins in the First Epistle to Corinth and runs through Jude, Peter and John to the Apocalypse. They are called variously the followers of Balaam and Cain. Both terms are illuminating. It will be seen, if the Old Testament originals are remembered, that we have in the Nicolaitans those who saw little ethical compulsion in the faith of Christ. They found, as some have always found, the standards of Christianity an irksome burden. In Corinth they frequented the temple of Aphrodite. Everywhere they attended the guild-feasts and sought to keep a compromising foot in both worlds. All this is suggested by the reference to Balaam with his doctrines of compromise. Cain suggests the bloodless altar, flower-decked, the mark and emblem of a religion void of moral sternness. Jude and Second Peter should be read by those who seek to understand the danger which lay in this vicious movement. Writing to Thyatira, John calls one of their leaders Jezebel. That name is redolent of a ruinous alliance between Israel and Tyre, a mingling of light and darkness, of God and Belial. Such were the forms of the pagan attack on Christianity—an intellectualism which emptied the gospel of its content and a libertinism which soiled its testimony.

The letter is something more than an indictment of emerging heresies. It has positive teaching to set forth as relevant today as in the first century. It is a vital and a living document of Christian worth and must be studied devotionally as well as theologically and historically.

First, let us look at what John wrote with the thought that he had error to contend with, wolves in sheep's clothing to watch and to frustrate, and a battle with false prophets which is as old as the Church of God. Secondly, let us watch for the author. A writer lives in his work. The man who rested on Jesus' bosom is worth knowing. There is a light about the head of those who walked with the Lord, like that which made the face of the old lawgiver shine. John has much to tell us of the race of God in the human heart. Thirdly, let us never lose sight of ourselves. This is the letter of John, but it is also the Word of God—quick and powerful. It has its own message for each of us.

The translation aims at fidelity. John is usually simple, sometimes rugged in his style, and occasionally obscure. It is not the business of a translator to expand or clarify the text. The English rendering shows some of the ruggedness and the occasional obscurity of the Greek, relying on the commentary to make the meaning clear.

The second and third letters of John are the shortest

letters in the New Testament. They give illuminating glimpses into the functioning of the early churches of Asia. Their ancient and original context would not have been considered important enough to retain and perpetuate had they not been from the pen of a revered and famous person. Like Paul's letter to Philemon, the single sheets of papyrus on which the two brief letters were written held the worth and sanctity of their writer. This in itself is argument for their traditional authorship.

The correspondences of language leave no doubt that both letters are from the same hand. To set the brief documents side by side is to be convinced that they were written not only by the same person, but during one session of dictation. Similarities of thought and expression are strong enough argument that the two personal letters were also by the author of the longer general epistle. Compare 1 John 2:7 and 2 John 5; 1 John 2:18 and 1 John 4:1-3 with 2 John 7; 1 John 2:23 and 2 John 9; 1 John 3:6,9 and 3 John 11.

The author styles himself the "Elder." It is clear from a remark of Papias, who lived from A.D. 70 to 146, that "the Elders" was a general term for the first generation of the leaders of the Church. John, the apostle, last link between the Lord and the Church in the closing decade of the century, was preeminently "John the Elder." There is no need at all to assume that "John the Elder" was any other person than the aged apostle. He was obviously a man invested with the greatest authority, visiting and supervising a wide circle of Christian communities. Much of the perverse attempt to disassociate the elder and the apostle dates back to Eusebius. The fact remains that Papias knew and talked with John and also with Aristion, a disciple of Christ. Even granting Eusebius' prejudiced strictures on Papias as an historian, it was a weighty responsibility to contradict such first-hand authority. The same Eusebius' remark that there were two burial places for John shown in Ephesus merely shows that there were two rival sacred sites, a not uncommon phenomenon. There are two "holy sepulchers" of Christ shown today in Jerusalem. The landing-place of Odysseus and the Phaeacian ship, turned to stone by the angry Poseidon, are found traditionally on both sides of Corfu.

The letters are real. The surprise of the vast mass of papyri discovered in Egypt has been the vast extent of ancient literacy, and the volume of the everyday correspondence between private persons on all manner of subjects of daily interest. The letters of the New Testament, although at times they touch the heights of literary power, have as their prime object information and exhortation in the plain and simple speech which the common people hear gladly. And the discovery of Egypt's mass of proletarian correspondence has shown the class of writing to which the letters of Paul, Peter, John, Jude and James belong. There is no perceptible difference between the style of the private letters of the first and fourth century. They are innumerable and repay the careful examination of the New Testament scholar. It is revealed that Paul observed with some care the forms of polite address common in his day. There is an opening word of salutation, followed by thanksgiving and prayer for the person or company addressed. Then comes the special subject of communication, greetings to friends, and perhaps a closing word of prayer.

The recipients of the second letter are "the elect lady and her children" (*KJV*). Much unnecessary difficulty has been made over these words. It has been suggested

12

that the phrase means a particular congregation. John, in such case, would be writing in the obscure language which he found necessary when he sent out the Apocalypse from his exile on Patmos. No such obscurity is very visible in the rest of the small letter.

Others, with even less likelihood, have suggested that the lady's name was "Eklecta" (elect). Electa was a common Greek name but Eklecta was not. "Lady," under the same theory, would be either a term of respectful affection (My Dear Eklecta) or, as in modern Greek, a mode of address like modern Mrs. Another rendering, perhaps the most likely, is to regard "Lady" (*Kuria* in Greek) as a proper name. There is authority for this in papyrus letters (and consider, "Lady Bird Johnson"). Thus the address would be, "To Kuria, my fellow Christian. . . ."

Someone has gone further and found in Kuria a reference to Martha, which bears the same meaning. Mary, the Lord's mother, was in John's care and it is far from impossible that she was still in his household in Ephesus. Could the Bethany family have similarly migrated there? Anyone who traces the wanderings of Aquila and Priscilla will be impressed with the mobility of the people of the first century. The fall of Jerusalem in A.D. 70 mightily dispersed the Church. Martha, an aged widow, could possibly be alive in John's day. However, this is fancy quite beyond proof.

At any rate Kuria, if such be the name of a real person, must be added to the list of noble and influential women who were members of the first century Church. She lived somewhere in western Asia Minor, and her house was no doubt the meeting place of local Christians like the home of Nympha at Colossae (Col. 4:15).

A sister of the lady addressed, and evidently dead at the time of writing, had a family in Ephesus. John writes to assure their aunt and cousins that they are earnest Christians. It was a time of intellectual unrest. Christians were confronted with powerful paganism, a state-sponsored religion, theological sabotage, and disruption within their own community. The situation is painfully recognizable and relevant.

The person addressed in the third letter is "Gaius, the beloved." It is impossible to say whether it is one of the names in the New Testament records (Acts 19:29; 20:4; Rom. 16:23; 1 Cor. 1:14). It was a common name. It was known in the Caesarian house from Julius to Caligula. It was incorporated in the Roman marriage ceremony (*Ubi tu Gaius, ego Gaia*—"Where you are Gaius, I am Gaia"). An old tradition, again beyond proof or refutation, names Gaius of Corinth as John's amanuensis on Patmos. He took down the Apocalypse and published it in Ephesus. It is also said that one Gaius was head of the congregation in Pergamum—a difficult assignment.

Gaius, at any rate a man of influence and authority, was having trouble with one Diotrephes, a rich layman. This person, leader perhaps of some such faction as those which rent Corinth much earlier in the century (1 Cor. 1:10-17) may have challenged John's authority. Or he may have been simply a domineering man, not uncommon in human situations, who liked to have his own way. A visiting group of evangelists was refused hospitality by Diotrephes, in spite of the fact that they had John's approval. The matter was reported at Ephesus. John sends the letter before us to Gaius, promising with some vigor that he will deal with the situation personally.

FIRST JOHN

WHAT IS THE MESSAGE WE PROCLAIM?

1 John 1:1-4

"We are telling you of that which existed from the beginning, which we have heard, which we have seen with our eyes, which we gazed upon, which our hands have felt, the life-giving Word. For the Life was made visible, and we saw it, and bear witness and testify to you of the Life, the Eternal Life which was with the Father and was made manifest to us—that which we have seen and heard, I say, we announce to you also, that you may have fellowship with us. Yes, and our fellowship is with the Father and with His son, Jesus Christ. And these things we write that our (less probably *your*) joy may be fulfilled." 1 John 1:1-4

Like the Epistle to the Hebrews, John's letter begins without a salutation. This in no way casts doubt on the traditional authorship. Perhaps the letter actually accompanied the Gospel in its first distribution, and everyone knew from whom both came and to whom they were addressed. John was a considerable figure, the elder statesman of the whole Church. His immediate diocese in Asia was considerable. His wider diocese was what men called the world.

John's elaborate repetition is the measure of his earnest desire to make his main point clear. It is exactly the type of emphasis employed in the prologue to the Gospel of John. His point is this: In the Gospel he had just given or is about to give to the Church, he has written of the Son of God, a Person of the Trinity who walked on earth in sinless beauty as Jesus Christ, the Lord and Master and Friend of those who knew Him; those of whom John was the last.

The apostolic gospel, he is maintaining, is no new

mystery open for free speculation, but a faith once given, clear-cut in its doctrine and founded on a divine and living Lord. There was point in the insistence. Varied heresies arose to afflict the early centuries of Christian witness. John's First Epistle, coming from an otherwise silent generation, is indication that later heresies first took shape in the first century. The Arians taught that there was a time when the Word was not, and the Docetic heresy maintained that the Lord's body was unreal. It was, at times, intangible. John's vigilant eye had marked the beginnings of both doctrines. In the hammering emphasis of these opening verses he leaves no doubt about the apostolic position. He was preaching a gospel based on a real, historical Christ, attested by eyewitnesses. He was handing on the truth that none might doubt that Jesus Christ was both Man and God.

This strong affirmation is without a doubt that which makes John's letter so relevant today with the current tampering with the truth of the historic Jesus, who was also the Christ of God. We have "heard" Him, he says, remembering a loved familiar voice. We have seen Him "with our eyes." And lest this is not enough he adds the stronger, more emotive verb of the prologue (John 1:14). We "beheld His glory." Then he remembers Thomas, in a scene burned on his mind (John 20:26-29). The disciples touched, handled, felt Him, no phantom as the foolish Docetists said, but flesh and bone. He lived, God made flesh, real, real, real.

All this was in order that they might have fellowship with Him and His. Those invited to such communion include all who read the words, from then till now. In the face of the disruptive tendencies which were beginning to gather head, John calls for unity. The Greek word translated "fellowship" in verse three of the *King James Version*, is not easy to translate. The word "communion" is specialized in ecclesiastical speech. "Fellowship" has become diluted in modern usage. "Partnership" suggests business. But partnership is what the word means, partnership in the great heritage of the apostles, a partnership with the intimacy of vine and branches, of body and members, the partnership of John 17:3,6,21,22,23.

He writes that "our joy may be fulfilled." Joy is envisaged as a consummation. Evil divides, scatters, shatters the fellowship of man with man. C.S. Lewis' imaginative picture in the fantasy of *The Great Divorce*, envisages the more demonic of the damned in eternal and accelerating flight from all others (p. 19ff.). In the "grey town" they move apart, disintegrate, hate. Christ draws together, unites, fuses each with each. Passions melt. The world sweetens. Would God the whole world did. It could "in Christ." That would be joy.

There is in Greek, as in English, a difference only of one letter between "your" and "our" and it is not surprising that manuscripts are divided. A scrutiny of the evidence does seem to lead to the choice of "our."

Both Epistle and Gospel, with Genesis in mind, refer to that unimaginable "beginning." Both speak of the Word—that Mind behind Creation which revealed itself in Christ, revealed itself in terms which men could understand and so grasp eternal life. "Seeing and hearing," "bearing witness," "life manifested," "joy fulfilled" are all concepts and language common in the Gospel. Prologue and Preface (John 1:1-18 and 1 John 1:1-4) bear all the marks of one mind, one proclamation, one writer.

2
WHAT DO
I DO
WITH SIN?
1 John 1:5—2:2

"And this is the message we have heard from Him and make known to you, that God is light, and there is no darkness at all in Him. If we say that we have fellowship with Him and go on walking in the darkness, we lie in word and in deeds. But if we are walking in the light as He is in the light, we have fellowship with one another, and the blood of Jesus Christ His Son cleanses us from every sin. If we say that we are not sinners, we delude ourselves and the truth is not in us. If we confess our sins He is faithful and just to forgive us our sins and to cleanse us from all wickedness. If, I repeat, we say that we have not sinned, we are making Him a liar, and His Word has no place in us."
1 John 1:5-10

Christianity, says John, is not a philosophy thought out and taught, a code conceived and published. It is a revelation, a message passed on. Its heart lay in the simple truth (John 1:4,5), that God is Light. The imagery is satisfyingly complete. Light penetrates the unimaginable depths of space. In all the vastness of the great globe of vanished millennia into which the telescope can probe, the gleaming galaxies float or tell in effulgent light how once they floated. The mind staggers before the thought of how long that light took to traverse the intervening space.

Without light there is no vision, no comprehension of reality, no confident journeying, no growth save of the chill, dank, uncanny things which grow in lightless caverns. In John's world the image of light, like that of water, was sharper and more powerful than it is today. The modern world has gone far to banish physical darkness. Darkness once was an enfolding menace, daylight a measureless benediction.

Light, like God, can exist apart from what it illuminates. On earth light is a medium, a means by which we see shape, color, objects. But light exists apart from that which it illuminates—as it is possible to realize on a high flight, with a blue cloudless dome above and a blue haze beneath blurring all clouds or earth. Light can be an environment, a wonder which fills an immensity of space. So one day we shall know God, not His afterglow, like Moses in the rock's cleft (Exod. 33:22,23), or even as we comprehend the reflection of His glory in Christ (2 Cor. 3:12-4:6). And remember that if darkness was a more palpable menace in those days, light was also more real and intense. No landscape was smogsmeared or blurred by the smoky breath of human industry. Distances stood sharp and clear in the mighty radiance. That is why there were temple towns like Baalbek, where successive waves of men worshiped the vast source of light, the sun, under varied names.

Why did John set this telling image at the head of his definition? Because Gnosticism was showing its head. The Gnostics were a group who became vocal and powerful in the second century. They sought to confine the deep things of the faith to a spiritually enlightened élite. Oddly enough, the moral and ethical requirements of the gospel sometimes weighed little with these sectaries. Conduct was indifferent. The body was a poor thing, a mere casing or envelope which could not contaminate an enlightened soul. To be enlightened, to understand truth as no others did, was the hallmark of spiritual aristocracy. The Gnostic attitude had clearly found its first expression when John wrote, and verse 5 is a direct and pungent reference to it. The so-called enlightened walked in darkness, for "God is light," and they dishonored Him.

"If we say." The small conditional clause comes three times like a hammer blow (6,8,10) and points out John's hatred of false profession. He had heard his Master utter the words of Matthew 23. He held in memory, if not already on papyrus, the claim of John 8:12. What Paul had written of such pretensions had long been a possession of the Church (Rom. 2:19). To walk meant habitually to live, and recalled a famous word of Isaiah (9:2). With the simple clarity of one who sees past and through all ambiguities, falsehoods and deceptions of life, he states that those who continue with lives unchanged and claim to have communion with a God whose touch transforms, are liars and deny truth not only by what they say but by the lives they live. Deeds can speak louder than any words. Evil deeds seek the coverage of darkness (John 3:19; Rom. 13:2) and John sees no other explanation of lives which contradict high profession of religion, save deliberate mendacity. The obligation to act out the faith professed still holds. There are absolutes for the Christian, principles beyond discussion, ethics not modified by situation, moralities beyond debate.

To live in the light of Christ, exposed to His presence in which no sin is easy, is to know what God's salvation is. "Walking in the light" has two blessed results. The first is fellowship with one another. The secret of all unity and happiness in the corporate life of a Christian group or society depends upon the quality of the spiritual life of the Christians who compose it. If they have fellowship with God, it follows that they cannot be at variance among themselves. Communion with our brethren is the consequence and indeed the evidence of our communion with God. The second result, also in verse seven, is cleansing. As *The Expositor's Greek Testament* remarks: "When we walk in the light, that demonstration of the length to which God has gone in sacrifice for our sakes, is ever before us, and the amazing spectacle subdues our hearts, takes possession of them and drives out evil affection."

There were those who saw no need to discipline the body and bring it into obedience to the faith professed, to demonstrate their faith by works as James had said with emphasis. There were also those who professed to be sinless (v. 8). The first group hypocritically denied that their misdeeds separated them from God, in spite of Isaiah's words (59:1,2). The second group denied the very presence of sin. Some tortuous argument was no doubt used to prove that the sinful nature in the enlightened was eradicated, or that sin was a matter of the body, while the true self—the spirit—was undefiled. Such claimants to sinless perfection have emerged more than once in the history of the Church.

John meets the contention with two statements. He first draws attention to the inherent corruption of the nature of man. Grace may be the medicine, potent and perfect, but recovery is a protracted process. There is no point, says verse 8 in leading ourselves astray. If we do so, "the truth is not in us," and truth in John's writings might be paraphrased "the revelation of the true God." In verse nine he speaks of the frequent falls of the believer and God's provision for them. Why shut our eyes, he pleads, to experimental fact? We sin, and it is our hope, joy, and strength to admit the fact. God is faithful and keeps His covenant (Ps. 89; Heb. 10:23). He is faithful to His nature, even though man wavers (2 Tim. 2:13). "I will forgive their iniquity," it stands recorded, "their sin I will remember no more" (Jer. 31:34).

In verse 9 there is one surprising word. Note that God is "faithful and just to forgive our sins." (*KJV*) *Just* is the word, not *merciful*. The forgiveness we have in Christ is based on God's justice, on His righteousness. God forgives not as a man might, because he chooses to be tolerant or indulgent, but because in the completeness of His plan forgiveness is consistent with His justice. Sinful men can believe in the forgiveness of their sins, not by convincing themselves that their sins are forgivable, but by their faith in the justice and consistency of God once for all revealed in Christ and His finished work. The conception is breathtaking. It is so far beyond anything man might imagine of God or goodness, that the heart can only bow in adoration before the clear vision of love revealed. In such light, how pathetically feeble does a human claim to sinless perfection appear.

That is why the chapter concludes as it does. The first heresy denied that sin came between man and God, the second that sin was a reality at all. Now come those who would admit that sin does alienate, who would concede that such propensities exist, but that they were not guilty. They simply had not sinned. Verse 10 might be written: "If we say that we have not sinned we make him out a liar, and God's revelation has no home in our heart." The perfectionism which is refuted in this chapter has two causes. The first is the stifling of the voice within, the turning of a deaf ear to the inward testimony. The second is pure ignorance of Scripture. Scripture states that all have sinned, and that doctrine is embedded in both Old Testament (1 Kings 8:46; Ps.

14:2,3; Isa. 53:6; 64:6) and New Testament (Rom. 3:23). If the Word is powerful and regnant in life, such error cannot raise its head.

"My little children, I am writing these things to you in order that you may not sin. And if anyone sin we have an Advocate with the Father, Jesus Christ the righteous. And He Himself is the atoning sacrifice for our sins, and not for ours only but for the whole world." 1 John 2:1,2

As he continues the old apostle turns from "we" to "I," and addresses his readers with the affectionate vocative which he is to repeat six times (2:12,28; 3:7,18; 4:4; 5:21). No one had a better right than the last survivor of the Twelve to look upon himself as the father of the family of faith. We who seek intimate study of the mind of John should note and seek in this letter the thronging echoes of the Gospel. Here he is remembering the strange, tense atmosphere in the room which Judas had just left, and the thrill of a voice on the beach of Galilee in the dawn twilight (John 13:33;21:5), and hearing again words which had haunted sixty years. "Little children, yet a little while I am with you. . . ." (KJV) How true that statement was for the last remaining member of that party. How well he was using those last rich years.

The aged should study John. The Venerable Bede used his last breath to dictate the translation of the Fourth Gospel. Something of the scorn of Tennyson's Ulysses for those "who store and hoard themselves," would bring back vigor and usefulness to many lives which have become too preoccupied with death.

26

"How dull it is to pause and make an end,
    To rest unburnished, not to shine in use!
    As though to breathe were life. Life piled on life
    Were all too little, and of one to me
    Little remains; but every hour is saved
    From that eternal silence, something more,
    A bringer of new things; and vile it were
    For some three suns to store and hoard myself,
    And this gray spirit yearning in desire
    To follow knowledge like a sinking star
    Beyond the utmost bound of human thought. . . ."

This Christlike tenderness precedes a warning. He would have his people know that there must be no surrender. He has insisted on the reality and sinfulness of sin in special reference to those who were making light of evil. He writes "that you may not sin," for nothing in his message must be understood as conferring a license to sin. He foresees a two-fold perversion: the notion that sin is an abiding necessity which "we must learn to live with" and against which strife is useless, and the idea that we may sin with license since we have Christ to cleanse us. John answers that the whole drift of his message is that we should not sin. In truth, we have forgiveness if we seek it in humble confession. The whole effect of true knowledge of God, God who is Light, should be to inspire a hatred of darkness and all that belongs to darkness, and all which finds refuge or comfort in darkness.

Yet John knows how hard is the way, and hastens to repeat what he has already said, "If anyone sin, we have an advocate." The tense in the Greek text is aorist with the emphasis upon the act of sin, not the state. "Sin not, but if any man sin . . ." the rapid transition places sin and its remedy in close proximity, as they are ever meant to be. Note that the writer passes humbly to the first person. He numbers himself with the weak and faulty.

This last word, another strong echo of the Gospel, needs attention. It is one of the best known Greek words in New Testament theology, although it occurs only five times, once here and four times in the Gospel (John 14:16,26; 15:26; 16:7). It is sometimes translated "comforter," but "advocate" is the only rendering which fits all the contexts. The word literally means "someone called alongside" with the implied meaning of help, especially in some court of law. In the Gospel it refers to the Holy Spirit, called alongside in Christ's place to woo us to deeper experience. Here it refers to the intercessor (Rom. 8:34) who pleads for His own in heaven. In John 14:16 that function of the Lord is implied. The Holy Spirit was to be "another" advocate.

How much better is this than the law. "He who fulfills one commandment," ran a Rabbinical tract, "has gained for himself one advocate" (the Johannine word is used). "He who commits one transgression has gained one accuser." If such were the case, as Jowett's hymn puts it: "How helpless and hopeless we sinners had been."

But now observe a difference. Our advocate, like some clever apologist in court, does not plead extenuating circumstances or seek with subtlety to put our case in the most favorable light. He acknowledges our guilt and puts forth his own redeeming sacrifice as the grounds for our acquittal. He is our "propitiation." Some have disliked the use of this term because it implies an angry God who required appeasement. The Old Testament had no doubt at all about God's anger against sin. No reader of the Gospels can be in doubt about the wrath of Christ against pose, hypocrisy and the use of holy things as a cloak for evil. The pagan gods were capricious, arbitrary, cruel, unpredictable. Both wrath and its appeasement assume different shape when God is perfect holiness, perfect justice, perfect love. And yet in justice sin had to be dealt with. Hence the plan of God's salvation. To make it clear, John chose a word from the religious vocabulary of his age. The Christian concept, mightily enlarging and transforming the word, carries its significance far beyond any pagan notion of ritual expiation or persuading, by some act of abasement, sacrifice or gift, a deity to relent. The transforming difference is that God initiates the process.

The final clause preaches no universal salvation. Christ's remedy for sin is simply available for all who will (John 1:29; 3:16; 5:24). There is no other possible propitiation. No man is excluded from participation.

3

DO MY ACTIONS MATCH MY PROFESSION?

1 John 2:3-11

"And in this we recognize that we know Him, by keeping His commandments. He who says: 'I know Him,' and does not keep His commandments is a liar and the truth is not in him, but whoever keeps His word, in this man truly is the love of God victorious. Thus we know that we are 'in Him.' The one who professes to 'abide in Him' is bound so to live as He lived."
1 John 2:3-6

In this passage John returns to the Gnostics, or at least to the group of pseudo-Christian philosophers from whom the Gnostics sprang. There was high talk among them of "knowing God," and being "in Him," mystically united on a plane denied to lesser intellects. Knowledge was the passion of the Greeks. Paul knew that fact well enough (1 Cor. 1:22). Knowledge and mysticism had united in Plato. Knowledge, in the speculations of that mighty mind, had been a path to heaven. That is why Platonism could never have become a gospel. Something nearer the heart, something wider and more simple was needed if the common people were to hear gladly. That is what came in Christ.

Now the incorrigible intellectuals were hiding God in words and entangling truth in speculation. They were claiming a knowledge which lay beyond knowledge, an understanding of God given in some mystic revelation in the ineffable experience of a chosen few. "Not yet are we able," wrote one of these dangerous dreamers, "to open the eyes of the mind and to behold the beauty, the imperishable, inconceivable beauty, of the Good. For you will see it when you cannot say anything about it. For the knowledge of it is divine silence and annihilation of all senses. . . ." So it has always been. God in reach of simple men, comprehensible in Christ, has been thrust beyond understanding and made into some intangible "Ground of Being," some "Ultimate Reality." Christ has not been accepted for what John said He was, God's final and complete revelation of Himself, His last saving word to man. Ancient error and new.

Such high-flown nonsense was not the gospel of Jesus Christ. But the danger was that the error found a basis in misapplied texts of Scripture. In the Old Testament, "knowledge of God" is represented as the goal and end of human aspiration. "Let him who boasts," said Jeremiah, "boast of this, that he understands and knows Me, that I am the Lord" (Jer. 9:24). It is not accident that in his Gospel and Epistle John boldly follows this theme. In both documents the knowledge of God is set forth as an attainable blessing.

John and the mystical heretics diverged in their teaching on the manner of attainment. For the Gnostics, or their ancestors of John's day, the knowledge of the Most High was a species of theosophy, divorced, as we have seen, from ethical religion, a mystical assurance denied to common men. For the apostle, knowledge of God was the experience of His love in Christ, the prerogative of great and small, of wise and simple, and the return of that love in obedience and upright living (John 15:15-24).

There is a debt of love and a binding obligation. The doctrine is tested by its fruit. So we prove the validity of religious experience. Unless that experience involves a reorientation of the will, a setting of the affections in the direction of the moral excellence revealed perfectly in the Person of the Lord, it is no true experience of

God. It is a sham, a futile stirring of the emotions, self-exaltation, and a pose.

"By this we know" (vv. 3,5) marks the test of genuine faith. It is a characteristic of the whole letter to supply norms, tests, proofs of what is authentic and what is sham. Such were the times and such the confusion that the old apostle saw. His last and most urgent task was to establish some fundamental rules. They still apply.

So ends a section of the Epistle. It deals mainly with a perversion of the Gospel, and lays down the rules by which true religious experience can be judged. In the midst of the section, and relevant to this theme, lies a passage (1:8–2:2) which reaffirms the Christian teaching on sin and forgiveness. And it does so in the first speech of the faith, which was derived from the Old Testament. It is easy to see why John was preserved alive until this latter day.

"Beloved, it is no new commandment I am writing to you, but an old commandment which you had from the beginning. The old commandment is the word which you heard. [*From the beginning* is omitted in the best MSS.] Again, it is a new commandment I am writing to you—a thing which is true in Him and you, because the darkness is passing away and the true light is already shining." 1 John 2:7,8

John begins with a vocative of love: "Beloved." The "brethren" of the *KJV* is a less well-attested reading. There is a commandment both old and new (Deut. 6:5 and John 14:23). The paramount necessity of love is an old commandment. It was the very essence of the gospel.

It was embodied in the very elements of the message "from the beginning." It was part of every discourse and action of the Lord. It was the fruit of the Spirit, and the most consistent lesson of experience.

And yet, it was a new commandment, and a touch of sadnes· haunts the phrase. The old apostle appears here almost to confess a life-long lack. In the evening of his ministry he had discovered the supremacy of love. In the synoptic Gospels where John appears, he is marked by all the characteristics of a passionate and fiery nature. "Son of Thunder," the Master called him. He was intolerant and self-seeking and for all the love which his Lord gave to him, John was not the figure whose gracious features are seen behind this Epistle.

When did the change take place? The "Son of Thunder" still lived at Ephesus. Irenaeus and Eusebius quote a story of the great Polycarp who sat at John's feet. The apostle once visited the public baths, and seeing the heretic Cerinthus there cried: "Let us flee, lest the building fall, since Cerinthus the foe of the truth is in it." This looks like the old John. When did the new man appear? Was it the slow erosion of the faults, which haunt the personality, by the blessed indwelling of God? Was it the exile on Patmos and the vision of his Lord which changed the character of his ministry? The day of suffering and withdrawal is sometimes the opportunity He makes or takes to teach a lesson long unlearned. Or was it the writing of the Gospel? Did that blessed urge, which sharpened thought and memory and moved his pen, bring back so gloriously those three years of fellowship that the aged man was changed and sanctified anew?

Let us, at any rate, draw two clear lessons from this moving passage. This first is that it is never too late to learn. It is true that the arteries harden and the mind stiffens in mortal man. It is also true that the Holy Spirit is not restricted and that the willing heart at any age can be illumined anew and delighted with fresh revelation. Note secondly that the fierce critic of Cerinthus lost none of his power by the change. In a new spirit of love he deals as faithfully with error as uncompromisingly as he ever did in the earlier ministry. And he deals more effectively with it. From the last years of John's ministry came the Fourth Gospel and the Epistles. The Son of Thunder could not have written them. The Lord waited patiently for him to age. When the darkness began to pass away and the new, true light began to shine, the Lord put a pen in His servant's hand. He set to work on his life's final and greatest task.

A last word on these verses. "True" is a favorite word with John. He had known what it was to follow furtive and fitful gleams. . . . He had misconceived Christ's kingdom. He had been alien to his Master's spirit. Now he saw truly, clearly, without blur or shadow. He knew what to do and did it.

"He who says he is in the light and hates his brother is in darkness still. He who loves his brother continues in the light and there is no cause of hindrance (or stumbling block) in him. He who hates his brother is in the darkness, and lives in the darkness, and does not know where he is going because the darkness has made him blind." 1 John 2:9-11

For the fifth time the clash between profession and conduct is dealt with. We have seen this presented as the antithesis of truth and falsehood, light and darkness. Now it is hate and love. They are opposites, like light and darkness. It is only a failure to understand the hyperbolical language of the East which sees a contradiction here with Luke 14:26. To hate one's father and mother is merely to hold them second to God.

The one who hates his brother, says John, is still in the darkness. No work of grace is yet manifest in him. Had it not already been said, "If I have the gift of prophecy, and know all mysteries and all knowledge . . . and do not have love, I am nothing"? On the other hand, the personality which loves contains no stumbling-block. There are three distinct interpretations possible for this phrase.

First, there is nothing in him likely to cause him to stumble, an echo of John 11:9,10. Second, if the more common meaning of *skandalon* (which we have translated "stumbling-block") is chosen (Matt. 13:41; 18:7; Rom. 14:13) the passage might mean "there is nothing in him to offend, or cause others to stumble." From the records of the early Church it is clear that the love of the Christian community was often a major commendation of the gospel. The absence of it, as most Christians are brought forcibly to realize, is a major cause of stumbling today.

The first clear mark of the disastrous change appeared in the fourth century when the pagan historian Ammianus commented on the religious controversies of the Church. "The enmity of the Christians toward each other," he remarked, "surpassed the fury of savage beasts against man." The third possibility is to translate "in it," rather than "in him." The forms are the same. "In it" would refer to the light. "In the light there is no chance of stumbling" is consonant with John 11:9,10. Perhaps

36

Psalm 119:165 was in the writer's mind. The word *skandalon* represents the Hebrew metaphor of "a snare" (Judg. 2:3; 8:27) and is a late form of *skanalethron* which in classical Greek means the bait-stick in a trap. The hater, the loveless, is necessarily outside God's plan, and fair game for the Evil One.

The choice would appear to be between the first two meanings with a balance in favor of the second supported by the last words of the verse. The man who cherishes hate incurs the penalty of spiritual and mental blindness. He chooses the darkness and the darkness penetrates the whole fabric of his being. Like the pit-pony of the cruel old days, the mole, and the fish of Kentucky's Mammoth Cave, the dwellers in darkness lose the faculty of appreciating the light. Unused powers atrophy. New Zealand's kiwi has the rudiments of wings, but never flies. Life in a forest which knows no wild animals or reptiles, and the abundant food of a land which was inhabited for countless centuries only by birds, took away the need for flight. The unused power died.

So with the mind, the heart, the spirit of man. Never love, and the capacity to love is lost. Worse than the loss of sight or flight is the loss of the ability to see spiritually. To lose the light in that sense is to lose the vision of God, and no deeper or more tragic disaster can befall the soul of man. How solemn and awful is the warning. When we allow hate to creep in, we drink deep of the poison, a poison which blinds and kills.

4

WHAT IS OUR RELATIONSHIP TO THE WORLD?

1 John 2:12-17

"I am writing to you, little children, because your sins are forgiven for His name's sake. I am writing to you, fathers, because you have come to know Him who is from the beginning. I am writing to you, young men, because you have conquered the Evil One. I wrote to you, children, because you have come to know the Father. I wrote to you, fathers, because you have come to know Him who is from the beginning. I wrote to you, young men, because you are strong, and the Word of God abides in you, and you have conquered the Evil One."
1 John 2:12-14

A new section of the Epistle begins here, running almost to the end of the chapter. The refrain on three vocatives and two tenses, has rhetorical importance. The apostle is about to make a searching and exacting claim. He pauses to assure one and all in his congregation that he addresses them not as worldlings, but as convinced and victorious Christians. The "little children" of verse 12 and the "children" of the next verse are probably general appellations subdivided into "fathers" and "young men," the older and the younger presumably in the faith. The whole classification is rhetorical and designed to form a pause of emphasis in the letter as the way is prepared for verse 15.

The change of tense in the two triplets is most plausibly explained as a reference to the Gospel, and such an explanation would assume that the Gospel was already written. To say that John suddenly remembered a small courtesy of Greek letter writing, and reverted half-way through a solemn passage to an "epistolary aorist," a past tense which sees the letter from the point of view

39

of the recipient, is psychologically unlikely. He points to the Gospel just written. We have frequently observed and shall observe again that the Epistle is best understood as an accompanying document to the Fourth Gospel.

John says in effect, "My children in Christ, young and old, I write now as I wrote before, in full knowledge that you are in Him, and what is more, walking intelligently and faithfully in Him, but there is one precept of surpassing importance which I must impress upon you. It is this. . . ." The appeal he proceeds to make is then based on forgiveness granted and accepted, on the knowledge of Christian experience, and the victory which strong cleansed hearts have won through the indwelling Word of God. The forgiven are not an "enlightened" elite, but the great and small, the young and old, who have laid hold by faith of Christ's salvation, have learned to know God, and in the act defeated the Evil One. John thus echoes the central theme of his Gospel when he addresses his audience as the people of the new covenant (Jer. 31:31-34), whose sins are forgiven, who know the eternal God (Isa. 52:3-6) and who have overcome the world. The passage is a tissue of echoes both of the Gospel and the Old Testament.

John is now ready with another of his sharp contrasts—the Church and the world. The world is what his people were facing in Asia. Laodicea had almost succumbed. Hence the challenge now to be made.

"Love not the world nor the things that are in the world. If anyone loves the world, love for the Father is not in him. Because everything in the world, the lust of the flesh, the lust of the eyes, and the proud glory of life, is not of the Father, but of the world. And the world and its lust is passing away, but he who does God's will abides forever." 1 John 2:15-17

The world of John 3:16, which "God so loved," is the human race in all its need. John uses the term for the rebel order, organized evil (5:19), almost the "darkness" of this earlier theme, the pagan society which pressed upon the Church from every side. How heavily it bore upon the individual is illustrated by the First Epistle to the Corinthians. It is difficult sometimes for us to grasp the pervasive nature of ancient urban paganism. Society was more closely knit, with less chance of privacy, individualism or withdrawal, than is our right today. Many pages in Tertullian reveal vividly the practical difficulties which at every turn confronted the Christian. "Why even the streets and the market place," he writes, "the baths and the taverns and our very dwelling-places, are not altogether free from idols. Satan and his angels have filled the whole world."

It was worse even than this. The conscientious Christian was forced to absent himself from public festivals and all manner of communal activities because proceedings were entangled with the ritual of pagan sacrifice. His membership of a trade-guild, and in consequence his commercial standing, goodwill and livelihood, involved the awkwardness of "sitting at meat which had been sacrificed to idols."

Here lay the real reason for the hostility to the Christians. The new religion struck at the root of social intercourse and threatened a time-honored fabric of society. It is natural enough that there were Christians who sought a way out. It is probable that the groups castigated by

Jude and Peter, those who were later called the Nicolaitans, were those who had worked out a form of compromise with paganism. In chapters two and three of the book of Revelation, John had already dealt with them sternly and perhaps the battle was won. At any rate, it is in a softer mood, or faced with a less urgent problem, that he now bids his little children withdraw from the world and all it contains. Again the echoes of the Gospel are thick. The world is Satan's dominion (John 12:31; 14:30; 16:11), he who spreads the miasma of his dire control over all. And along with its prince, the world is doomed (John 12:31; 16:11).

John proceeds to detail. There is first the lust which the flesh feels, the desire for unlawful indulgence. Temptation teemed in the ancient world. For all the evil of today and the flaunting of temptation, for all the rapidly deteriorating situation in the vast urban conglomerations, the modern city is not as shockingly seductive in its wickedness as was Corinth or Ephesus with its temples served by courtesan priestesses. The law in the world of the twentieth century, at least professes to reflect the sanctions and restraints of Christianity. Evil in John's day was less bound in its activity. Then comes "the lust of the eyes." Tertullian emphasizes the spiritual ruin wrought by the circus and the theatre. Similarly Augustine, quoting this passage, remarks: "This is that which works in spectacles, in theatres, in sacraments of the devil, in magical arts, in witchcraft—none other than curiosity." The modern parallels are obvious to everyone, the scribblings of pornography, the sex-ridden cinema, the increasing boldness of television carnality, with the very advertisements sodden with degraded sexuality.

Then comes "the proud glory of life," the braggart

42

boast of life, the glamor of what men think splendid or however one may render it. The word is not easy to translate. The corresponding personal noun occurs at Romans 1:30, and 2 Timothy 3:2 in the sense of boaster. There is an amusing passage in the *Characters* of Theophrastus, an Athenian of the fourth century before Christ, which illustrates it at length. It runs:

"The Boaster is the kind of person who will stand on the jetty and tell complete strangers how much money he has at sea, and discourse on the magnitude of his investments, his gains and losses. . . . If he enjoys company on the road, he is likely to tell how he served under Alexander, how he got on with him, and how many jewelled goblets he brought home, and to discuss the Asiatic craftsmen, how much better they are than the European—though he has never been out of Athens. He will say that he was granted a permit for the export of timber, but did not use it to avoid ill-natured gossip, and that during the corn shortage he spent more than $50,000 in gifts to the poor. He will be living in a rented house but will tell anyone ignorant of the facts that this is the ancestral home, but he is going to sell it because it is not big enough for his entertainments."

Reduced to human proportions such was the boaster as the whimsical eye of Theophrastus saw him. The boastfulness of life contained all this and more. John sees it through more searching eyes. It was the ostentation of the rebellious human heart, the flaunting of paganism, and the self-advertisement, esteem and confidence of unregenerate men.

Commentators have pointed out that the threefold

43

classification includes all sources of sin and is illustrated by the temptations of Eve and the Lord. First, "the lust of the flesh": Compare, "every tree that is . . . good for food," and "command that these stones become bread." Compare, secondly, "pleasing to the sight" with the spectacular display of "throw yourself down." Lastly, compare "the tree of the knowledge of good and evil" with Satan offering "all the kingdoms of the world, and their glory." (Gen. 2:9; Matt. 4:3,6,8). Genesis, the Gospels, and John cover the spheres of common temptation—uncontrolled appetite, false values, and exaltation of self.

All this, says John, is passing away. It is in the very act of dying, a transient and moribund sham. He that does the will of God has linked himself with eternity. And how true! How fixed and permanent the world order seemed to privileged Anglo-Saxons at the turn of the present century. What flux, change, and impermanence has life seen since then. It was always visible to the seeing eye. Francis Lyte saw "change and decay" when he paced the Devon beach in 1840. The essential transience of civilization has come to be accepted as an established fact. With fierce acceleration the world changes. It never seems to change for the better.

Only those who stand apart from it, who contract out of it, are immune from what is called, among the maladies of secular society, "future shock." Insofar as lust and pride enter into the texture of a society or a way of life, to that extent are they self-destructive. The only escape from its wheel of death is by union with God, the permanent, the eternal. "O Thou, who changest not, abide with me." J. B. Phillips renders the passage well: "For the whole world system, based as it is on men's primitive

44

desires, their greedy ambitions and the glamour of all they think splendid, is not derived from the Father at all, but from the world itself. The world and all its passionate desires will one day disappear. But the man who is following God's will is part of the permanent and cannot die" (2:15-17).

5

HOW CAN I TRIUMPH OVER FALSE TEACHING?

1 John 2:18-28

"Children, it is the last hour, and just as you have heard that Antichrist is coming, even now there are many antichrists; whence you may recognize that it is the last hour. They withdrew from us, but they did not belong to us; had they belonged to us, they would have remained with us; but they withdrew, to make it clear that they are not, any of them, of us." 1 John 2:18-19

Nothing is so damaging in the study of New Testament prophecy than to imagine that the eternal God, who stands above and outside of time, is bound by the clocks and calendars of men. "It is the last hour," says John. Because he wrote those words almost nineteen centuries ago there are those who might imagine he was wrong. Note carefully that it is not enough to ask simply what John himself meant. A prophet who is truly inspired can utter words whose sense and meaning transcends the conceptions of his own mind. In the widest signification John was indeed writing in "the last hour." The only event in world history which can equal the first entrance of God into human history, the Advent of His Son, is His Second Coming. And what are twenty centuries compared even with the age of a finite universe, itself the creation of an eternal God? Calvin said correctly: "He calls that 'the last time' in which all things are being so completed that nothing is left except the last revelation of Christ."

John based this solemn warning on the contemporary fact of mounting apostasy. There is little doubt that he had in view the self-styled enlightenment, preached and propagated by Cerinthus and his school. They were "antichrists." The word is interesting. The New Testament is clear about the coming danger of "false Christs." As we trace the theme through the book, we become aware of the emerging reality of one supreme figure who sums up in his grim person the characteristics of all satanic opposition to the Lord. (See Matt. 24:5,24; Mark 13:22,23; Acts 20:29,30; 2 Thess. 2:3; 2 Pet. 2:1.)

For all this the actual word "antichrist" occurs only in the first and second of the letters of John (2:18,22; 4:3; 2 John 7). The next occurrence of the term outside the corpus of Scripture is in John's disciple Polycarp, a fact which helps to establish the Johannine authorship of the Epistles. The word means more than "false Christ." It conveys the idea of a counterfeit, a rival, a usurper, "a kind of diabolical parody," as Dodd puts it, "of God's Messiah." [1] And how vividly in the world of deified dictators and Marxist evangelism can we echo John's words.

The antichrists, John proceeds to say, were nominal members of the Church but never really part of it. How could they be, accepting as they did "a lie"? Dodd remarks, "The supreme enemy of Christ's redeeming work is radically false belief." The quaint old notion that it does not matter what a man believes so long as he leads a decent life needs no confutation in a world buzzing with ideologies. The conflict between Christ and antichrist is fought out upon the field of the mind. "We do not war," says Paul, "according to the flesh. . . . We are destroying speculations and every lofty thing raised up against the knowledge of God, and are taking every thought captive to the obedience of Christ" (2 Cor. 10:3-5).

John was not prepared to regard the purveyors and entertainers of deadly heresy as the members of Christ. Such was his position. "They withdrew," he says, "to make it clear that they are not . . . of us." We are reminded of a phrase common in the Fourth Gospel, our continual standard of reference in the exegesis of this document, the phrase "that the scripture might be fulfilled." We should consider its meaning. God did not send the Holy Family into Egypt in order to fulfil a prophecy. In His divine overruling of events He permitted the flight, and the fulfillment of the prophecy emerged in the outworking of a vast plan which allows no evil to frustrate it. So here. The heretics left the Church in anger and bitterness. They thought to build something greater, and in pursuit of a perverse design abandoned the Lord's people. Paul had warned the Ephesian elders of such people (Acts 20:29,30).

Out of evil God brought good. The secessionists were seeking their own wicked advantage. It turned out that they fulfilled a plan of God whereby the truth was protected. Falsehood declared itself and withdrew. In calm confidence that nothing could baffle the protective love of the Father, John abbreviates the process with a simple clause of purpose. It was all providential. In the Greek text there is nothing to justify the "no doubt" of the Authorized Version. It arises from an attempt of Tertullian to render a Greek particle which needs no special rendering, and which merely marks potentiality. The mistake found its way into the Vulgate and has been dogging English versions since Tyndale and Cranmer. The Authorized Version is also incorrect in the last clause.

"But you have an anointing from the Holy One, and you all know. I did not write to you because you are

49

ignorant of the truth, but because you know it, and because every lie is contrary to the truth. Who is the real liar but the one who denies that Jesus is the Messiah? This is the antichrist, the one who denies the Father and the Son. Everyone who denies the Son, neither has he the Father (and the one who confesses the Son has the Father also)." 1 John 2:20-23

From the serious subject of his last discussion, John turns with an expression of confidence in his reader. "But you," he says, "have an anointing." They were blessed and enlightened by God's Holy Spirit, enlightened not after the fashion of the high-minded heretics, but by the very spirit of the Lord. Notice that we have replaced "and" by "but." Greek frequently failed to distinguish between the copula and the adversative, and it is often necessary to mark the fact. An example is, "be angry and sin not," where the obvious meaning is "be angry *but* sin not." That is, "Let your anger never be other than righteous anger." A difficult charge!

Note, too, that "anointing" is "chrisma." The assonance between this noun and its derivative "Christ" would be striking to a Greek reader. John says there are many antichrists, but there are also many who know that anointing which gave Christ His title. Anointing, in the Old Testament, was a rite of consecration. The Hebrew "Messiah" and its Greek translation, "Christos," meaning as they do "the Anointed," underline the priestly function of the Lord. Along with their Lord, Christians share this privilege. "He who establishes us with you in Christ," writes Paul, "and anointed us is God, who also sealed us and gave us the Spirit in our hearts as a pledge" (2 Cor. 1:21). In these verses Paul makes a similar, almost punning play on *Christos* and *chrisas,* as John does on *chrisma* and *Christos.*

Note another important detail. In both verses 20 and 27 the pronoun "you" is emphatic. "But you have an anointing . . . ," says the first text. "You too have an anointing . . . ," says the second. Why? It seems clear that the Gnostics, whose teaching is never far from John's thought in this Epistle, claimed and perhaps practiced a special "anointing." A Gnostic document says, in the obscure language the heretics often affected, "We alone of all men are Christians, who complete the mystery at the third portal, and are anointed there with speechless anointing." Probably the sectaries had adopted some of the rituals of the pagan mystery-religions, and were in the habit of exalting their ritual over the simplicities of John's little flock. Fear not, says the apostle, your anointing is real.

In verse 20, note that "all" in the best manuscripts is the subject of "know" not the object. "You all know (the truth)," not "You know all things." The former reading given by John against the self-styled enlightened, remains in the text as a rebuke to sacerdotalism. We are all "priests of God," equally entitled to the Spirit's insight.

The next verse underlines this fact. John's approach is simple. He has warned his friends against antichristian falsehood, not because they lack intelligence, but because they possess the truth, and because every species of falsehood is alien to the truth. The *Cambridge Greek Testament* quotes Maurice: "Many of us think we can put the truth into people by screaming it into their ears. We do not suppose that they have any truth in them to which we can make appeal."

51

"Who is the liar?" asks the apostle abruptly. And who is he? Surely the one who tells another monumental lie, who distinguishes, like Cerinthus, between Jesus and Christ, and thereby denies the Incarnation, denying the Father along with His Son. Study Matthew 11:27; John 5:23; 14·′, 15:23. The central truth of John's Gospel was the unity of Father and Son. Only through the Son can the Father be known (John 1:18). To deny God's revelation in His Son is to shatter the whole of Christian truth and to stand in fundamental opposition to the whole doctrine of the atonement. He who does this is in very truth the Antichrist. There are still those who speak of the fatherhood of God and yet deny the deity of Christ. Whatever such a religion may be called it is not Christianity. These two verses condemn its heresy in comprehensive terms. "Everyone who denies the Son loses all claim on the Father, and [continuing with the words found in many important manuscripts] the one who confesses the Son has the Father also."

And is it not true that the hundred cults of diluted and perverted Christianity which delude the unthinking today begin with a damaged Christology, a diminished, dethroned and attenuated Christ? No one comes to the Father, understands God, has any communion with the Most High, save those who come through the Son, who has shown what He is like (John 1:18).

"As for you, that which you have heard from the beginning, let that abide in you. If what you have heard from the beginning abides in you, you yourselves will abide in the Son and in the Father. And this is the promise which He Himself made us, Eternal Life. These things

I wrote to you concerning those who are trying to lead you astray. But as for you, the anointing you have received from Him abides in you, and you have no need for anyone to teach you, but just as His anointing is teaching you about all things, and is a true anointing, and not a lie, even as it has taught you, abide in Him. And now, little children abide in Him, so that when He is made manifest, we may have boldness and not be shamed from His presence at His appearing."
1 John 2:24-28

In verse 24, says the *Cambridge Greek Testament*, "the arbitrary distinctions introduced by the translators of 1611 reach a climax." The same Greek word is translated in three different ways in one verse, "abide . . . remain . . . continue." Elsewhere it is rendered in four other ways, making seven English words to one Greek: dwell (John 6:56; 14:10,17), tarry (21:22,23), endure (6:27), be present (14:25). This inconsistency is to be regretted. The idea of abiding is characteristic of John in all three divisions of his writings, and should be translated uniformly and consistently by one word. Here he says in summary: "Let the truth which first brought you to salvation dominate your thought and feeling. In such case you will remain in spiritual union with the Father and the Son." Or perhaps the order is significant. John says "the Son and the Father." stressing the thought that by abiding in Christ we abide in God.

This is eternal life! Eternal life is not a duration of being, dating from death through eternity, but a quality of living, available for the existence of earth and necessarily indestructible because it is the life of God. Such is His promise, says John, using for the first time a word common in Paul and Luke. Here, too, is a plea for conservatism. There is no new gospel, adaptable to the context of time and place. The faith is anchored firm and deep in Christ. Let no preacher of novel doctrine deceive them. And was there ever a time when the Church more needed this strong warning. The day of itching ears is on us, for as Paul warned, "they will accumulate . . . teachers in accordance to their own desires" (2 Tim. 4:3).

In verse 27 John returns to his confidence in his readers. They need reminding rather than teaching. They have an anointing, a confidence God-given, a fruit of committal (John 7:17), the inner persuasion of "the Spirit of truth" (John 15:26; 16:13). The words are not to be taken as an expression of anti-intellectualism. The whole letter proves that instruction in Christian truth is necessary. It is false intellectualism that the apostle has in mind, and Ephesus was rife with it.

Verse 28 is a practical conclusion. Somewhere sometime, we shall all meet the Lord. And in what spirit shall we meet Him? Let it be with the fearless trust with which a child meets his father, not "shamed from His presence." The phrase contains a picture of shrinking form and averted face. The word "boldness" literally means "freedom of speech." By implication it means the calm confidence which is unabashed, able to speak openly, and free from all dissembling, reticence, cr deceit.

Let Phillips' felicitous rendering close the section. Let us so live consciously in Him, "that if he were suddenly to reveal himself we should still know exactly where we stand, and should not have to shrink away from His presence" (2:28). The conception, in its ancient setting, is amazing. "Bold I approach the eternal throne," wrote

Wesley, and how can man so presume? The very monarchs of earth could not be approached with boldness, much less with the freedom of speech which lies in the Greek word. Esther would have died when she appeared unbidden in the throne-room of the vile Ahasuerus, had he not in grace extended his sceptre towards her. No pagan god was thus accessible. Even the God of the Old Testament was approached with ritual of sacrifice, and His holy of holies trodden with awe only on the sacred occasion.

But John speaks of an open door, a way for any justified sinner to tread. Says the writer to the Hebrews "by virtue of the blood of Jesus, you and I, my brothers, may now have confidence to enter the holy of holies by a fresh and living Way . . ." (Heb. 10:19, *Phillips*). And let us be ever mindful of the privilege and, open though the way is, not tread it with irreverent, noisy or ungrateful feet.

Footnote

1 C.H. Dodd, "The Johannine Epistles," *Moffatt New Testament Commentary* (Edinburgh: Hodder, 1946), p. 48ff.

6
WHAT KEEPS US FROM SINNING?
1 John 2:29—3:12

"If you know that He is just, you know that everyone who practices righteousness is born of Him." 1 John 2:29

This verse forms a transition to another section of the letter ex*nding, with one major digression (4:1-6), to 5:12. Dodd divides at 4:12, making 4:13 to 5:12 another main division, and the suggestion is not without logic. It is a fact that, through the rest of the Epistle, the thought of God as living love is dominant. By a gentle change we pass with this verse from the antithesis of light and darkness to that of love and hate, from the opposition between God and the world to that of God's children and the same hostile system. The theme of love naturally introduces that of God's family. The fellowship of the first half of the letter becomes the personal relationship of the latter half. The "walking in the light" of the first two chapters becomes the "practicing righteousness" of the later theme.

This is not to imply mere repetition. New subjects also intrude—the Second Coming, Christian courage, and divine sonship. Generally the theme traverses old ground by new, rich paths, setting truths already stated in new light and new contexts and with new emphasis reinforcing the old appeal. Can Christian preaching do more?

The prime purpose of 2:29, this verse of introduction and transition, is to stress the fact that practical righteousness is the fruit and the sign of the holy relationship which is to be the theme. It is no matter of mysticism divorced from life's conduct. The child of God demonstrates his standing by the visible simplicities of Christ-like living. God the Father, as John has been insisting since he wrote the prologue to his Gospel, cannot be separated in thought from Christ the Son, who set Him forth in terms men could see and understand.

Note the identification which is implied in the two pronouns, He and Him. *He* is Christ. Tennyson's phrase, "our fair Father Christ," is not a repugnant idea, but it is not a scriptural one. John's first pronoun undoubtedly refers to Christ. The *Him* of the last phrase demands reference to God the Father. As in 2:27, John takes the oneness of the Trinity for granted. He quite naturally thinks of the Father simultaneously with the Son. Our sonship depends wholly upon our standing in Christ. Christian sonship is of grace not of right. Paul's quotation of the pagan poets (Acts 17:28) does not imply, as he himself amply shows, any countenance of wider ideas. In Old and New Testaments, revealed truth teaches that man becomes God's child by processes which spring from God's love and God's grace.

"See what unearthly love God has given us, that we should be called (as indeed we are) the children of God. This is why the world does not recognize us, as it did not recognize Him. Beloved, we are the children of God now, but it has not yet been made clear what we shall be; but we know that when He is shown forth we shall be like Him because we shall see Him as He is. And everyone who has this hope built on Him, purifies himself, just as He is pure." 1 John 3:1-3

The translation given above of the interrogative pronoun is a trifle bold. It meant originally "of what country?" as though the user sought a category in which to place some person not like anything else in his familiar context. "What sort of love is this?" asks John, as though unable to identify what place could bring forth a beauty so surpassing in its strangeness. See Matthew 8:27 where the uncanny calm on Galilee called from the overawed disciples the same wonder. And see 2 Peter 3:11 where the same pronoun challengingly appears.

The first words of chapter 3 thus strike the keynote. In the section concluding with 5:12 the word "love" occurs sixteen times as a noun and twenty-five times as a verb. It appears five times as a verbal noun. The conjunction may be taken quite literally, as a conjunction of purpose. Love, this unearthly love, has a purpose "that we should be called the children of God." In other words, the Johannine idea of rebirth and the Pauline idea of adoption meet and fuse here. There could be no conceivable method or device whereby sinful beings attain such a state or such a privilege save by the exercise, the operation, and the will of a power unimaginable in its strength and its unearthliness. It is all of love and grace, not of right and birth.

Moreover, the purpose is consummated. "As indeed we are," says the apostle. The words are omitted by the manuscripts followed by the Authorized Version, under the leadership of the Tyndale and Geneva translations. The authority for the words is overwhelming. Justin Martyr quoted this verse with "and we are" in place, revealing beyond controversy that he knew the Epistle. (Born at the turn of the century, Justin died in A.D. 165.)

John then proceeds to a more somber note. The blind world sees nothing unique in the Christian. But what of that? The same world hated and crucified Christ. And is the servant greater than his Master? Can the child of God expect more justice or discernment from mankind than man gave to God Incarnate? There is pathos in the phrase. The persecutions of Nero were over. Since Nero's day the Christians had been a proscribed sect. Persecution had been intermittent under Vespasian. Titus ruled briefly, and then came the tyrant Domitian, third and last of the Flavian family. Rome called him "the bald Nero." Persecution became a pursued policy again. It was under Domitian that John's flock suffered and he himself found exile—or protective custody, on Patmos. The governor of Asia must have been a senator, and the senatorial class of Rome had as little cause to love Domitian as the Christians did.

Beyond this life and whatever it contains of glorious privilege, there is something wider and more glorious. From the sixth beatitude onward, the vision of God recurs as a New Testament promise, and the logic of John's simple prophecy follows. To see God would crush and shatter the sinner. But the Christian is a child of God and has confidence before his Father's face. The great day of meeting will be a day of transformation when the rags and tatters will fall away and the blessed shall be clothed fitly for the presence of the King.

They have a blessed hope "built on Him," says verse 3. John perhaps echoes the quotation in Romans 15:12, and the similar phrase in 1 Timothy 4:10. With quick application John turns to the present and the practical. Lest his followers become too other-worldly, John reminds them of the natural conclusion. Let those who one day shall be like Him, live in the light of the fact.

"Everyone who practices sin practices also lawlessness.

And you know that He was revealed to take away our sins, and sin does not exist in Him. Every one who abides in Him does not continue in sin. Every one who continues in sin, has not seen Him nor come to know Him." 1 John 3:4-6

The Authorized Version obscures the antithesis between verses 3 and 4. The writer is emphasizing what he has just said by giving its opposite in an expanded form. In consequence "everyone" must appear in both verses, and since the contrast goes further back, the same verb must be used in 2:29 and 3:4. Practicing righteousness and practicing sin are set in opposition. The word is not the happiest of translations. It does bring out the fact that it is habitual action, a set attitude, that John has in mind, not the occasional fall of the believer.

Sin and lawlessness are set forth as convertible terms. The sinner acts as if no law exists to limit human conduct. Such a law does exist and a stark and simple view of sin is part of the profession of Christianity. The reality can be lost in jargon but to the Christian there are stark alternatives, to obey or not to obey the will of God. The Gnostics claimed that they were above the moral law, uniquely enlightened. They turned freedom into license. God's children have a law, not a code of Sinai, but the will of the Father. Verse 5 reminds them of the central fact, which it is salutary for them ever to remember. Christ came to deal with sin—past, present, and future. John uses the very word he heard John the Baptist use by the Jordan River those many years ago (John 1:29). The sinner disregards both His work, stressed in the first half of the verse, and His example with which the verse concludes.

Verse 6 requires careful interpretation. On the face of it there appears to be a flat contradiction of the doctrine expounded earlier in the letter (1:8—2:2). It may be assumed that the writer saw no such contradiction. The early fathers had various explanations. Augustine says, "To the extent that he abides in Him, a person does not sin," and proceeds without justification to limit sin to lack of brotherly love. Montgomery's rendering seems to accept Augustine's point, "Whoever continually abides in Him, does not habitually sin."

There is no real contradiction if the present tenses are insisted upon. The present tense of a Greek verb implied habit, continuity, unbroken sequence. It is this tense we have endeavored to render by the use of the verb "continue." The believer sins, and John has both admitted the fact and named the remedy. Opposition to sin and hatred of it is the ruling principle of his life. He fails, but the enemy has no rejoicing. The fallen rises again, confesses his fault, and presses on (Mic. 7:8). The habitual sinner does none of these things. Just as the apostates who had left the Church proved they had never really belonged to it, so the determined sinner who "continues in sin," covets no change, and seeks no victory, proves that he has never really known Christ.

Thus the verse finds explanation. There is no contradiction involved, but it may be admitted that the words deal with a spiritual clash of which every Christian is conscious; the contradiction between his conduct and his aspirations, his achievement and his ideals, between the Lord he owns and his attempts to be like Him. Paul put it into passionate and revealing words (Rom. 7:14-25).

"Little children, let no one lead you astray. The one who practices righteousness is righteous even as He is righteous. The one who practices sin belongs to the devil for the devil sins from the beginning. That is why the Son of God was revealed, to undo the works of the devil. Every one who has been born of God does not practice sin because God's life abides in him. And he cannot continue sinning because he has been born of God. In this the children of God and the children of the devil are distinguished. Everyone who does not practice righteousness is not of God, and neither is the one who does not love his brother. For this is the message you have heard from the beginning that we love one another. Not as Cain who was of the Evil One and murdered his brother. And why did he murder him? Because his own deeds were evil and his brother's righteous." 1 John 3:7-12

John has the true teacher's appreciation of the value of repetition. His method is the continual and varied confrontation of his people with the same truths, the same doctrines. Every man who faces week by week the same congregation knows the value and the necessity of such didactic method. And yet it is to be noted that John's repetitions are not mere reproductions of something said before. They always introduce new facts, new angles.

Verse 7 turns sharply with sudden reference to the false teachers. John tells his "children" that the very conduct of the sectaries was their sufficient condemnation. Their persistence in sin (v. 9) and their lack of brotherly love (v. 10) was sufficient proof that they had missed the prime purpose of Christ's very incarnation (v. 8). It was all so very plain. Sophistry and pride were making religion a difficult business, whereas it was and is still a matter for the simplest understanding. Truth and falsehood, right and wrong, God and the devil can never be reconciled. To know God means to stand in clear opposition to evil in all its shapes and forms. Sin is doing wrong. Righteousness is doing right. So, "let no one deceive you." John brought the faith of Christ within the reach and comprehension of the humblest slave in Ephesus. In the translation we have tried to bring out the force of the present tenses which interlace the passage, and which the Authorized Version tends to neglect.

Some details of interpretation remain to be cleared up. What does "from the beginning" of verse 8 mean? Some half dozen explanations have been advanced, only two of which are satisfying. The words either mean from the beginning of sin, or from the beginning of human life. The latter of these two seems more probable. There is no time in the record of spiritual history when man was not subject to the assault of the tempter. It goes back to the beginnings of history. It is woven with the story of Eden.

Christ came to pull the devil's work to pieces. The same verb is used in Matthew 5:19, and John 5:18 of loosening a bond, or relaxing an obligation. In John 2:19 it is used of pulling down the Temple. It is a vivid and colorful word. Christ disintegrates in life the vast edifice which Satan has built on this invaded planet.

Genetics provides the key to the meaning of verse 9. In the moral sphere, as verse 10 astonishingly asserts, a free-willed being can choose his parent. We have the right (John 1:12) to become the children of God, or to reject this privilege and become the children of the devil. With the choice goes that trend and tendency which comes of parentage. How conscious we all are at times of the strain and pull of hereditary forces. Innate and undeveloped possibilities are ours at birth. But there is a *new* birth. A new nature may be implanted. When Nicodemus came to talk to Jesus, in covert allusion to Ezekiel 36:25-29 and the strange dream of the valley plain where the bones of the dead came to new life, the Lord spoke of the necessity of a new life.

A man becomes what lies at the core of his personality. To entertain evil at the center of the being is to be consumed by it. The host of hate, falsehood, pride, becomes the thing he cherishes. Evil cannot be contained. It seeps into thought, word, action. It consumes the personality until the true self is dead and the evil implant becomes the whole. So, too, with God. Set Christ at the heart's center and He cannot be contained. He permeates thought, word, action until He pervades and revives the personality. He becomes the person He fills. Unlike evil, He does not destroy or kill. His presence is life. The indwelling Christ remakes, renews. Paradoxically, the host becomes more truly himself and is transformed into what God intended him to be. This surely is what is meant by carrying within one's person the living, regenerative seed of God. If a person with life so implanted falls into sin, he cannot be happy in the unnatural state. Christ within constrains, challenges, rebukes and presses hard on the conscience.

It might be noted that John took for granted the existence of a malign power of evil, a being dedicated to perversion, but for a time tolerated by God for some reason beyond mortal understanding. The fact that the last of those who walked with Christ held such a conviction is not to be lightly passed over. He had known One who had a forty-day adventure in the arid crags behind Jericho. There is a possibility that the reference to Cain touches one of the most diabolical heresies of the early centuries. Some authorities are of the opinion that the Gnostic sect of the Cainites can be traced back to the first century. This group of heretics taught some shocking doctrines. Matter and its creator, they maintained, were evil, and the revolt of Adam and Eve was the justifiable overthrow of a tyranny. It was the beginning of man's redemption, and Satan became a redeemer. With hideous consistency they identified Jesus with the Old Testament tyrant and maintained that He justly died for the evil He sought to establish. It followed that everything taught in the name of the God of the Bible was wrong. Cain, the Sodomites, Esau, Korah and such were heroes to be emulated, and Judas was a saint. What moral corruption flowed from such perversion can be well imagined. "The deep things of Satan," of which John speaks in Revelation 2:24, may have reference to this quite hideous perversion. We have the authority of Irenaeus for the practice of unnamed shame by these base sectaries in the name of God and for salvation. How evident such wickedness was when John wrote his letter we do not know, but the story of Cain is oddly prominent in the chapter before us.

7

HOW DOES JOHN DESCRIBE LOVE?

1 John 3:13-24

"Do not wonder, my brothers, if the world hates you. We know that we have passed over from the realm of death to that of life because we love our brothers. The one who does not love his brother remains in the realm of death. Everyone who hates his brother is a manslayer, and you know that such a one has not eternal life abiding in him. We have come to know what love is because He laid down his life on our behalf, and we should lay down our lives for our brethren. Whoever has this world's goods and observes his brother in need, and shuts up his heart from him, how can God's love abide in Him?" 1 John 3:13-17

Mention of Cain and his murder raises the subject of hate and its antithesis, love. Love is the reflection of God in His creation. The rebel world which shuts out God, shuts out love as it shuts out light. All that is left is hate and darkness. It should cause the Christian no wonder that the denizens of hate and darkness look on him as they once looked on his Lord. For solace he should turn inwards and contemplate the new society into which he has been born. There, says John, is love. Love which flows from Calvary, sacrificial, merciful. The Christian, says John, has migrated from one realm to the other. Cain was the first identifiable citizen of the devil's realm, Abel was the first to suffer because he belonged to God. The Lord gave warning (John 15:18-25; 16:1-3; 17:14).

We are thus faced with a challenging picture of the Church as it should be, a community knit by the bonds of love. Membership has one sign and certificate, the love of Christ outworked in practical brotherliness. It was a happy division of verse and chapter which gave the New Testament this second "John Three Sixteen." Lest Christian love should lose itself in starry thoughts of martyrdom, John brings it firm-footed to earth with a simple and practical illustration. A heart untouched by a brother's need makes idle claim to love. The petty sacrifice and self-denial which no crowd cheers, and none see with applause, is more often the acid test of reality than the spectacular renunciation.

It remains to discuss the abrupt introduction of the subject of murder. In chapter 8 of his Gospel, John told an incident which appears to have been again in his mind when he wrote the words we are now considering. It described a typical exhibition of the world's hatred. The Jews of Jerusalem were snarling hostility about Christ, and proceeding even to the ultimate wickedness of attempted murder. They claimed to be Abraham's children. With language hard to parallel, the Lord lays bare the hollowness of their pretensions. "If you are Abraham's children, act as Abraham did; but you seek to kill me. If God were indeed your Father you would love me. Rather you belong to your father the devil and seek to do his desires—he who was a murderer from the beginning" (John 8:37-47).

It may be imagined that as John wrote of the two worlds, the world of death from which the Christian has "passed over" (v. 14) and the world of life into which by faith he has moved, he saw the scene in Jerusalem almost a lifetime earlier. Here they stood, the two races, the children of God and the children of the devil. Life and death, light and darkness, love and hatred, such were the antitheses. Cain (v. 12) was a murderer because he was of his father the devil, seeking the fulfillment of his father's lusts. The Jews, ranged against their rejected Messiah, were of the same ancestry, recognizable by their deeds. All history is the record of the twain, of those whose breath and touch is death, and of those whose vibrant life begets its like.

With such forces ranged, is it a wonder that the world hates an utterly committed Christianity?

To approach history from any angle is to meet the same somber truth. How consistently is man in his mass the enemy of the good. The mob in the Jerusalem street yelling for Barabbas, Pilate washing coward hands, and the priests murdering a man for the safety of religion, form a group which is typical in history. In Greece, four centuries before that event, Plato had foreseen the situation. "The Just Man will be scourged, racked, thrown into chains; he will have his eyes burnt out and after enduring every pain he will be crucified." The familiar pattern had been for a lifetime before John's eyes. "Crucify him, away with him, not this man but Barabbas, he has a devil, a gluttonous man and a wine-bibber." Then said Mr. No-Good, "Away with such a fellow from the earth." "Ay," said Mr. Malice, "for I hate the very looks of him." Then said Mr. Lovelust, "I could never endure him." "Nor I," said Mr. Live-loose, "for he would ever be condemning my ways." "A sorry scrub," said Mr. Highmind. . . . The smell of burning flesh, the reek of man's intolerance for man, fills history. Man will not have before his eyes the reproach of human goodness, if by stone or stick or sword he can dash it from sight. And those sunnier generations which have imagined that such evil has at last been purged, have ended always like our own in sharp and rude awakening.

It is the measure of the old apostle's calm that, from

this contemplation of God's battle lines, he could make his chief emphasis the utter need of the Christian to demonstrate his care by a life of love outpoured.

"Little children, let us not love with words and with the tongue, but in deeds and in truth. Then we shall be sure that we are of the truth, and shall reassure ourselves before Him whenever our heart condemns us, because God is greater than our heart, and He knows all things. Beloved, if our heart condemn us not, we have confidence before God, and we receive from Him whatever we ask, because we keep His commandments and do those things which are pleasing in His sight. And this is His commandment that we should believe in the name of His Son, Jesus Christ, and love one another even as He commanded us. He who obeys God's commands abides in God, and God abides in Him. And it is through the Spirit He gave to us that we know that God abides in us." 1 John 3:18-24

This section, something of a digression and full of echoes of the Gospel, recapitulates many points already made in one form or another. It might almost be supposed that John set down in note form several themes for his messenger to expand verbally with reference to the Gospel which was already in the hands of those to whom he wrote. A. S. Way, in his preface to Paul's letters, suggests that such a practice might account for the difficulty presented by some of the more compact passages in the documents. "The bearer of the letter," he writes, "always an intimate friend of the writer, sometimes his amanuensis, would probably be familiar with its contents beforehand, might well have heard the Apostle's comments upon it, would possibly be entrusted with supplementary verbal communications, and so would be prepared to explain difficulties, to expand condensations, and to supply any links of thought that might be required."

The passage under consideration is not at all obscure or difficult. Way's suggestion may explain the cluster of clear references to the Fourth Gospel which fil! verses 22 to 24. The writer obviously meant this part of his letter to close with emphasis upon areas of teaching with which his audience was familiar. In abbreviated style with clear allusions to doctrines he had expounded elsewhere, he trusted responsible commentators in the church communities he addressed to make his meaning clear.

The first four verses require more detailed examination. Verse 18 is a comment on the practical piety enjoined in verse 17. We should love, as Bunyan puts it pungently, with something more than "the lick of the tongue." True love influences action. True love begets serenity of conscience. It is natural for a true Christian to sense some misgivings. There are dark days when the way is hard, failure obsessive, and the spirit burdened. Verse 19 touches the sincere misgiving of the spiritual Christian and assures him of the witness within. "Am I loving, as I should love?" he asks. "I love my brethren in Christ," comes the Spirit-prompted answer, and the doubting self-distrustful heart is reassured. God, who is greater than conscience, will also acquit, comfort and confirm. "He knows all things," the light against which we sin and the depth of our repentance. John is obviously promoting assurance, and his words must find interpretation in the context of his aim.

Verse 21 continues on to tell us that, if our heart does not condemn us, we have confidence in the presence of God. We approach him like children and not like criminals. We have already (2:28) dealt with the word translated "boldness," and pointed out that its basic meaning is "freedom of speech." Dodd quotes aptly from the *Conversations* of Brother Lawrence, who said that "when he had failed in his duty, he only confessed his fault, saying to God: 'I shall never do otherwise if you leave me to myself, 'Tis you must hinder my falling and mend what is amiss.' And after that he gave himself no further uneasiness about it. That we ought to act with God in the greatest simplicity, speaking to Him frankly and plainly, and imploring His assistance in our affairs just as they happen."[1]

This "simple, plain frankness" is very near to the meaning of the Greek word of verse 21. *Parrhesia* is quite difficult to cover by any one English noun. Confidence, to the Athenian citizen in the great days of the democracy, was the right to speak his mind. Without that he felt something less than free, and damaged in his morale. Christ gave us the right to speak without fear or shame to the living God. The wonder of it passes expression. How poised, sane and fearless, in the mad and frightened world the Christian should ever be. In such relationship with the Father, verse 22 continues, children who are obedient to His behests will not ask what He is likely to refuse. And so John moves to his conclusion with the familiar theme of the all-importance of conduct. He has insisted strongly enough on correct belief and on love. Both are illustrated by action, and the moral character begotten of our faith. We may possess all manner of enlightenment, but there is no spiritual union with God without obedience shown forth in righteousness.

He needs to make only one commandment. There is only one commandment we need to keep. "We should believe in the name of His Son, Jesus Christ." It follows that if such a one bade us love one another, we must do so. That is how we maintain our unbroken fellowship with God.

Footnote

1. Dodd, *op. cit.* pp. 92,93.

8

HOW DO I DISCERN THE COUNTERFEITS?

1 John 4:1-6

"Beloved, believe not every spirit but test the spirits whether they be of God, because many false prophets have come into the world. Recognize the Spirit of God by this: every spirit which confesses that Jesus is Christ come in the flesh is from God, and every spirit which does not confess Jesus is not from God. This latter is the spirit of antichrist of whose coming you have heard and which is already in the world. You, my little children, belong to God, and you have prevailed over such people, for He who is in you is greater than he who is in the world. They belong to the world; they talk its language and the world listens to them. You belong to God; he who knows God listens to us; he who does not belong to God does not listen to us. Thus we recognize the spirit of truth and the spirit of wandering." 1 John 4:1-6

Paul's teaching on prophecy is a useful commentary on this passage. Before the New Testament with its full and final revelation was in the hands of the Church, truth was revealed by "prophecy" or inspired teaching. In modern usage the word prophecy means rather fore-telling the future, and it undoubtedly often carries that meaning in the Bible. In the New Testament it bears a second meaning, "telling forth." The Church, without the complete body of divine truth, was dependent upon the men of insight who carried their fellow Christians to further depths of understanding.

It is a fact of sad experience that evil counterfeits the good, and the later chapters of the First Epistle to the Corinthians reveal certain aspects of the problem which prophecy presented. There were those who rashly and those who viciously claimed the prophet's inspiration. By

John's day the latter group had become a menace. There were teachers of heresy, never truly Christians (2:19), who claimed to speak with divine authority. They were really pagan (4:5). What they taught was pagan in its tone, and found acceptance with the pagan world. They sought to reinterpret Christianity in a form the world would accept. To this end they stripped the message of the offending cross, and reduced the divine Christ to human stature. We are not without acquaintance with their spiritual descendants.

When John wrote the letter we are studying, at the close of what we may call the New Testament era, this group was in the process of separating from the true Church. A century follows in which the documents are few in number and our knowledge scanty. Toward the end of the second century the evidence becomes plentiful again. The victory of which John spoke with such quiet confidence (4:4) is almost won. During the dimly lighted years of the second century it is not unlikely that the true faith fought with its back against the wall. John's words of warning, guidance, and encouragement with which the canon of the New Testament closed, must often have been on the lips of the faithful. John's writings were a vital addition to Scripture.

Those words of warning, guidance, and encouragement are also very relevant today. It is impossible to deny that there are spiritual influences loose in the world which do not emanate from God. Their power is sometimes vast and devilish, and too obviously evil for any Christian to doubt its source and nature. Often, as in the case of John's own perverters of Christian truth, error comes in the guise of enlightenment arrayed for the deception of the very elect.

"There is urgent need," says J. R. Stott in his scholarly Tyndale commentary, "for discernment among Christians. We are often too gullible, and exhibit a naive readiness to credit messages and teachings which purport to come from the spirit world. There is such a thing, however, as a misguided charity and tolerance towards false doctrine."[1] Hence the sane advice and the test John now sets out. Such spirits we must test. "Beloved," says John, as he said earlier in tender care for those whom he knows and pities in their bewilderment, "test the spirits." He uses a word he uses nowhere else which suggests a good and hopeful aim, a proving, with the desire that the object proved may stand the test. The other New Testament word for testing or proving, the one found in such sinister contexts as Mark 8:11 and 10:2, suggests the hope that what is proved or tested will be found wanting. The optimism in the test contains the essence of Christian love.

The basis of the test is nonetheless clear and firm. It is the full deity of Jesus Christ, God's Anointed in the flesh appearing. By this standard the Gnostic heresies of John's day and a host of heresies today stand exposed and refuted. It is a strange and significant fact that almost every deviant form of Christian faith in some way diminishes or distorts the Person of Christ. The test is so simple. Was Jesus truly God's Messiah, the Word made flesh, most truly man and most truly God? If not, whoever or whatever the source of the denial, neither person nor cult can claim to be called Christian. He was either God in flesh appearing or not worth consideration, much less worship. Perhaps it is worthwhile at this point to quote a well-known remark of C. S. Lewis in one of his famous radio talks:

"I am trying here to prevent anyone from saying the really silly thing that people often say about Him: 'I'm ready to accept Jesus as a great moral teacher, but I don't accept His claim to be God.' That's the one thing we mustn't say. A man who was merely a man and said the sort of things Jesus said wouldn't be a great moral teacher. He'd either be a lunatic—on a level with the man who says he's a poached egg—or else he'd be the Devil of Hell. You must make your choice. Either this man was, and is, the Son of God, or else a madman or something worse. You can shut Him up for a fool, you can spit at Him and kill Him as a demon; or you can fall at His feet and call Him Lord and God. But don't let us come with any patronizing nonsense about His being a great human teacher. He hasn't left that open to us. He didn't intend to."[2]

In verse 3 an interesting variant appears in the Latin Vulgate. It runs, "Every spirit which separates Jesus is not of God." The verb would allude to the separation of the Lord's true deity and humanity, and would refer to the teaching of Cerinthus. We cannot be guided by the aptness or suitability of a reading in our choice of a text. The assessment of manuscript evidence is almost a task of arithmetic. It is a bald fact that all the Greek texts are against the Latin reading. We have already referred to the writings of John's pupil, Polycarp, and the proof they contain that he knew this Epistle. Polycarp makes a clear reference to the text before us, and his reference supports the reading we have translated above.

The section closes on the note of apostolic authority which was conspicuous in the opening verses (1:1-4). No such tone can be adopted outside the New Testament. Apostolic authority was not delegated. There was no arrogance here. This man had walked literally with Christ. He had peered, in the murk of the morning, into the empty tomb. He had preached the gospel for a lifetime. He had suffered for the faith. He was the last alive who knew all the facts. When such a man dismissed those who opposed him as enemies of God, he could do so in God's name.

Footnotes

1. John R. Stott, "Johannine Epistles" *Tyndale Bible Commentaries* (Grand Rapids: Eerdmans Publishing Co., 1964) p. 153.
2. C. S. Lewis, *Mere Christianity* (New York: Macmillan, 1964) pp. 52,53.

9

IS LOVE
IMPORTANT?
1 John 4:7-21

"Beloved, let us love one another, for love belongs to God, and everyone who loves is born of God and knows God. The one who does not love has not come to know God for God is love. In this was the love of God revealed to us that God has sent His only begotten son into the world that we might live through Him. Love lies in this, not that we loved God but that God Himself loved us, and sent His Son to be an atoning sacrifice for our sins. Beloved, if God so loved us we too should love one another. No one has ever seen God, but if we love one another God abides in us and His love is made perfect in us." 1 John 4:7-12

The movement of John's theme has been likened to the proverbial windings of the river Maeander near which he lived. For all its intricacy and turning on its course, it has beginning and progress and safe exit to the sea. Someone has described John's mode of writing as spiral. The course of thought does not move in a straight line. It is like a winding staircase, always revolving round the same center, always recurring to the same topics, but at a higher level. A little patience is sometimes needed to follow it. No great literature, much less the Word of God, ever yielded its best to the hasty and impatient reader. Observe the tissue of references to the Gospel.

The transition from verse 6 to 7 may seem abrupt, as if an unpleasant subject had been summarily dismissed. The links are there for the finding. The power to love and the faith which confesses Christ, are both given by the Spirit of God. The antichristian spirit is selfish, exalts man, and divides the Church.

Such a quest was the tenor of John's ministry. Jerome's

story is well known: "Saint John the Evangelist, living in Ephesus in his extreme old age, when he was with difficulty carried into the church by his disciples, had no strength for longer exhortation, but could only say: 'Little children, love one another.' At length, the disciples and bret^l en who were there, wearied by the repetition, said: 'Master, why do you always say this?' He replied in words worthy of himself: 'Because it is the Lord's command and if that alone is done, it suffices.' " It suffices because God is love supremely, and only those who are partakers of the divine nature by faith can truly love. "Love one another," as an exhortation (v. 7), as an obligation (v. 11), and as a hypothesis (v. 12), runs like a theme through the paragraph.

In verse 8 John makes the third of his great pronouncements about God. "God is spirit" (John 4:24); "God is light" (1 John 1:5), and now, "God is love." Of the three great truths the last is chief. It shows the Spirit to be personal. It fills His glory with a warmth and life which brings it near to the heart of man. The idea has conquered the world and colored non-Christian thinking. The savagery, the terror, the cruelty and caprice of pagan theologies have been banished. Indeed, a subtlety of temptation today lies in the attitude which presumes on the love of God and forgets God's justice and stern condemnation of sin. Fitzgerald's Omar touches the note in a quatrain from his version of the Potter's Shop: The Pots speak and,

"Said one—Folks of a surly tapster tell
And daub his visage with the smoke of Hell;
They talk of some strict testing of us—Ah!
He's a good fellow and 'twill all be well."

All of which is far removed from the mighty truth

of John's immortal sentence. The love of God is the love of Christ, and when that is said all is said.

It is wrong to state that the idea of God's love was unknown in the Old Testament. The love of a father and husband appears in too many figures for anyone to believe that the Jew of the old dispensation had no inkling of the truth which became clear and glorious in Christ. It is true that in the New Testament the love of God became the dominant theme, all-embracing and complete. And in the New Testament, as if for last and final emphasis, the closing words stressed and restressed the idea. John was closing the canon, and closing it characteristically. In no book of the New Testament does the noun "love" occur so often as in the two and a half chapters which open with chapter 3, and in no book of the New Testament does the verb "love" occur half so many times as here. The very fact that God created man, the fact that He left man free to choose, the truth of redemption, pain, the blessed hope of immortality, are explained by love. God must be more than intelligence, more than justice. He is love, and the truth infuses, penetrates, and enlivens all other truths.

Verse 10 contains the deepest truth in this passage. "Love lies in this, not that we loved God, but that God Himself loved us." In the higher forms of Greek mysticism the notion of a God of love appears. The God of those great minds, Plato and Aristotle, was not a God who bends in love to sacrifice and save. Rather, He was the object of man's love, the goal and aim of the upward striving of enlightened souls. And that love with which the seekers struggle upwards, urgent to win the vision glorious, was nothing more than the sublimated emotion of man's human affection, of *eros*. The New Testament uses a different word, a word which in non-biblical Greek was cool and colorless. Paul and John took it and transformed it, filling it with the loveliness which no philosopher had imagined and firing it with a truth which man could apprehend only in the face of Christ, God's Son. Faced with the wonder of a God who loves us, how small is the demand that we love each other. The verb John uses in verse 11 literally means "to owe." "Beloved," says John, using that address for the sixth and last time, "we too should love one another." "We owe the world," says an old saying, "a debt of tolerance." Christianity goes farther than that. Love is tolerance in the right place, stripped of compromise with evil, active, seeking, redolent of the Lord, the gift of Love, who came to minister.

"This is how we know that we abide in Him and that He abides in us, because He has given us a portion of His own Spirit; and we have seen and bear witness that the Father has sent the Son to be the Saviour of the world. Whoever confesses that Jesus is the Son of God, God abides in him and he abides in God, and we know and have believed the love of God for us. God is love, and he who abides in love abides in God, and God abides in him." 1 John 4:13-16

The last division of the letter extends from 4:13 to 5:13. In John's usual fashion the section is not clear-cut. His style is conversational. He writes as one might speak with reaffirmations and effective emphasis. We can observe, as we read, the progress of thought toward great statements of truth and the development of a major purpose.

John's purpose was to build firmly in the hearts of Christian men and women, shaken and bewildered by a crop of noisy heresies, a strong assurance of salvation. In the closing verses of the third chapter he had begun to speak of assurance and confidence. He turned aside to discuss the true witness of the Spirit and its counterfeit. This digression led him to a further statement on divine love. Now, at 4:13, the theme of 3:24 is resumed.

At this point let us step very carefully, for we are at the heart of the apostle's message. The theme of abiding which has haunted his mind since that dark betrayal night is on his pen again. It is the inner witness of the Spirit which gives assurance, a deep awareness of a divine presence in the life which is not reached by mere logic, but comes rather by a conviction wrought of God and tested by experience. Such is the meaning of verse 13. Verse 14 links such assurance with the central article of the Christian faith, and verse 15 maintains that the genuine voice of the Holy Spirit in the heart issues in testimony to the saviourhood of Jesus Christ.

John was as aware as we are of the danger of an emotional mysticism. It is perhaps significant that in verse 14 and John 4:42 are found the only two contexts where John uses the word Saviour. In both cases the phrase "of the world" follows. The Lord came not to be the Saviour of an enlightened elite, but of all who would believe. The will, its opposition or surrender, is the test, not the presence or absence of a spurious culture. Assurance can be yours and mine, his yonder and the other's, of all who accept the gift which is for all, from a Holy Spirit who is no respecter of persons.

There is another sign by which the indwelling Spirit reveals His blessed presence, and that is by love. "He who abides in love abides in God, and God abides in him." The English of this rendering is unhappily weak and lends itself to inadequate interpretations impossible with the firm and powerful language of the Greek. We have described how the New Testament took the word *agapé* and filled it with a strong new meaning. It was as though the Spirit of God, casting aside the words which human fault had marred, took and sanctified a term, setting it apart for holy use. To "abide in love" contains no touch or taint of the sentimental. It certainly does not mean that anyone who feels for another a liking, attraction, or affection, is by that fact in living union with God. It is clear in John's writings that the phrase involves three conditions: to continue to live as the objects of God's love; to continue to love God; and to continue to love our brethren. As Dodd aptly puts it: "The energy of love discharges itself along the lines which form a triangle, whose points are God, self, and neighbor; but the source of all love is God, of whom alone it can be said that He *is* love."[1] This great and noble verse is the central thought of the Epistle. In it is the secret of fruitful living, the source of assurance, and the basis of all morality.

"In this lies the perfection of our love, in fearlessness on the day of judgment, because in this world we are living as He lives. Love has no fear in it, but perfect love banishes fear, for fear is connected with punishment; the one who continues to fear has not reached the perfection of love. We love Him because He first loved us. If anyone says: 'I love God,' and hates his brother, he is a liar, for the one who does not love his brother whom he has seen, how can he love God whom he has not seen? This commandment we have from Him, that he who loves God is to love his brother also." 1 John 4:17-21

Verse 17 is not easy to translate. More literally it might run, "In this fact love is made complete with us—namely that we should have confidence on the judgment day, because as He is we too are in this world." The meaning is that absence of fear is the measuring-rod of love. The ground of such confidence is the amazing truth that we are to God what the Lord was to His Father in the days of His flesh. If faith can once grasp this last mighty privilege, fear dies in the light and glory of it. If we stand clothed in Christ, no condemnation can touch us. The confidence and fellowship which exists between a true and loyal son and a good and loving father find perfection in the union of God the Father and God the Son. It is such union, such fellowship, which is offered the Christian. This blessedness can be broken only by our defection, our wavering. To abide in love is to live as Christ lived, and no terror can touch a soul so blessed.

Fear, says verse 18, has to do "with punishment." Fear *is* a form of punishment, the penalty which like some virus finds harbor in the sick soul. There is no worse torment, as the spirit of antichrist which stalks the world well knows, than utter terror. The thought of judgment beyond the grave is the sharpest of all fears. There was a Roman poet, writing a century and a half before John penned this letter, who sought in the name of Epicurus' philosophy to banish God from the universe. There are passages in Lucretius' somber poem which become morbid and hysterical with the terror of judgment to come, a terror which it was the prime object of his verse to uproot and efface from his own mind and the minds of men. To be rid of fear, the obsessive, paralyzing, spoiling malady of the human mind is the greatest blessing that the Christian faith has to offer. It is a blessing so great that too often we fail to lay hold of it and possess it, to enjoy it and weave it into experience.

Judgment is too clear a fact of history and experience to be dismissed in this fashion. There will be judgment on the rebel race, but the whole plan and purpose of the atonement was to save the believer from such condemnation. It is the clear insistence of John's Gospel that the child of God has naught to fear at his Father's hands. In the verses before us the same truth reaches sublime expression. Before such possibilities language falters.

In verse 19 there is an interesting variant. "Him" is omitted by a few manuscripts of first rate authority: "We love, because He first loved us." The love of God gives us the power to love. The thought of the amazing love of God revealed in Christ is the inspiration of all the love which stirs our hearts. We love, and therefore cannot hate. Such is the shining standard set before us. And no commentator can wrestle with themes so transcendent without a new surge of conviction that something divine is before him, unimagined and uncreated by men.

Footnote

1. Dodd, *op. cit.* pp. 117,118.

10
IS MY
LIFE
A VICTORY?
1 John 5:1-12

"Every one who believes that Jesus is the Christ, has been born of God; and every one who loves the Father loves that which has been born of Him. This is how we know that we love those born of God, by loving God and keeping His commandments, for the love we can bear God means keeping His commandments, which are not burdensome, for everything that has been born of God conquers the world. Our faith is the victory which has conquered the world. Who is the one who has conquered the world if not the one who believes that Jesus is the Son of God?" 1 John 5:1-5

The division between chapters 4 and 5 of the letter is not a natural one. In fact 4:19 to 5:5 forms a self-contained section of the argument. On a superficial reading the theme might seem repetitive, but closer attention will reveal John's purpose in this re-emphasis of truths and tests of reality already expounded. He feels constrained to meet the diffidence of the Christian who pauses after reading 4:18 to ask, "Do I, who so often feel the grip of fear, love God as I should?"

The answer is simple. In the practical, almost homely manner, which was his natural style, John shows that love for fellow Christians is the clearest and most convincing of demonstrations that we love God. Obedience to God's commands reinforces it. Love for God is the inner principle, love for the brethren is its outward manifestation. Love that does not include the desire to please and to obey is not worthy of its high name. This was the point of Leigh Hunt's well-known poem of the "angel writing in a book of gold." Verse 2 literally runs, "By this we know that we love the children of God, whenever we love God and keep his commandments." And such commandments, unlike the commands of scribe and Pharisee (Matt. 23:4), are not burdensome.

Whenever we love and obey we deepen faith and assurance. The opening words of the verse are a converse of 4:20 and 21, and are intended to suggest once more that love is not a mere matter of emotion. Just as love for God is demonstrated by obedience to God's command, so is love for God's people. If it merits its name, such love demonstrates itself in active benevolence rather than in passive profession.

And such love runs counter to the whole current of a godless world. The pressure of society upon the Christian is ever towards selfishness, and the fulfillment of the desire of the flesh, the desire of the eyes, and the proud glory of life (2:16). John has assured his children that there was a power in the Church greater than the demonic impulse which made the strength of paganism (4:4). Speaking now of the individual's strife and victory, he repeats the assurance. "Every common day," wrote C. S. Lewis' mentor, George Macdonald, "he who would be a live child of the living God has to fight the God-denying look of things." But "He who is in us" is the One who overcame the world. If faith can but compass that thought what can prevail against the Christian?

The way to victorious living is not the assertion of our better selves. A godless world order, the vast complex of temptation which arises from a society constructed on the principles of selfishness, and the pull and tug of evil within, weaken before the faith which looks to God and God only and remembers that He loved us first.

Note that verse 4 says "whatever is born of God."

The neuter is used, not the masculine, as though to cover and obliterate the human person. It is all, all of God. It is not the man, but what has taken place in the heart of man that wins the day. The participle is also a perfect participle. This verbal form in Greek contains the two ideas of something done in the past and a state resulting from that action and extending into present time. The participle contains not only the notion of the rebirth through which the child of God has passed, but also of the abiding life which follows that experience.

Verse 4 seems inexhaustible. The word *pistis*, which is the commonest word in Greek for faith, occurs nowhere else in the Epistles and Gospel of John, in spite of the pervasive presence of the idea. In its classical Greek form the word for victory occurs nowhere else in the New Testament. But it is not such peculiarities of vocabulary that make the wonder of the verse. It is the profundity of the thought that faith *is* victory. Once faith is born in the Christian's heart, he becomes forthwith invincible. If a man grasps with full confidence the truth of verse five, that the living God burst into human history in Christ and in Christ wrought his salvation, neither angry despot, leviathan, nor Satan himself can destroy him.

Consider the audacity of such a statement in its context of time and place. Familiarity has dulled the edge of some of the sharpest words in the vocabulary of the faith. An effort of the mind is required to catch the fresh strength of what is said. John, the fisherman from Palestine, wrote these words at the end of the first century of the Pax Romana. That peace was the gift of the great Augustus to the world, and it still held for all the omens of strife which had followed Nero's ending. Rome ruled the world in which the apostle lived and wrote, Rome, the mighty conqueror, whose word was law in all the deep rim of lands round the Mediterranean. If victory was the prerogative of any man, it belonged to the prince by the Tiber whose legions were probing for a firm frontier north of the Clyde and the Forth, manning the banks of the Rhine and the Danube, and containing the powerful Parthians behind the Armenian mountains. Rome was supreme.

But Rome was doomed. Already, in the cryptic language of the strange book he had sent to the churches of Asia from his exile on the island of Patmos, John had told of her defeat. The victory was theirs in whom Christ dwelt, who, outliving their persecutors, were the true guardians of the future. Faith, "the assurance of things hoped for, the conviction of things not seen" (Heb. 11:1) was to prove a mightier force than the swords of the legions and all the power of the vast organization of the Empire of Rome.

The clash with the Church, which began after the Great Fire of Rome in July A.D. 64, was Rome's supreme act of folly. Paul had hoped to win the great world system for Christ. Rome, commonly wise in dealing with the ways and faiths of those she ruled, had chosen to persecute the Church. It was a death-wish and a conflict which need never have been. Such a fatal choice has more than once been made by nations. It is made daily by individuals.

"This is the One who came through water and blood, Jesus, the Anointed; not through water only but through water and blood, and the Spirit is witness to this fact, for the Spirit is Truth. Because three are they who bear witness (in heaven, the Father, the Word, and the Holy Spirit; and these three are one; and three are they who bear witness on earth), the Spirit, the water, and the blood; and these three are in accord. If we accept as valid the witness of men, the witness of God is greater; because this is the witness of God, that which He bore to His Son. He who believes in the Son of God has this witness in his heart. He who does not believe God has made Him a liar by refusing to believe the witness that God has given us eternal life, and this life is in His Son. He who has the Son has life; and he who has not the Son has not life." 1 John 5:6-12

It may be well, before commenting on these verses, to clear the ground. It will be noticed that certain words, roughly corresponding to verse 7 in the Authorized Version, are bracketed in the translation given above. This is because they quite certainly form no part of what John wrote. Even a commentator as firmly orthodox in his textural criticism as Dr. C. I. Scofield remarks in the margin, "It is generally agreed that verse 7 has no real authority, and has been inserted."

The facts are that the rejected words are found in no Greek manuscript of the New Testament of earlier date than the fourteenth century, in no ancient Greek writer, in no ancient version of the Scriptures other than the Latin, in no early manuscript of the old Latin version, or of Jerome's Vulgate. They are first quoted as part of John's text by Priscillian, the Spanish Gnostic heretic who died in A.D. 385. Erasmus omitted the passage from the first printed Greek Testament of A.D. 1516, but undertook to introduce the words if a Greek manuscript containing them could be produced. Unwisely, he did not specify a manuscript of ancient worth and authenticity. He was faced with a late and inferior manuscript which did contain the passage. Against his considered judgment he kept his promise. So by way of Erasmus' 1522 edition, the interpolation invaded the text of the Greek Testament. The action of the Revised Version in cutting out the spurious words was a tardy act of justice. We should treasure every word of the inspired record, but we want no invasion of that record by the additions of men, however well-intentioned the theology may be.

Those interested in the methods of textural criticism might also care to consider the internal evidence. The following points might be made. First, the inserted words break the thread of the argument with an awkward parenthesis. Secondly, only once in a passage where the words are not closely linked, does John speak of "the Father" and "the Word" together. He either says "God" and "the Word," as he does four times in the first section of his Gospel and at Revelation 19:13, or he links "the Father" and "the Son" as he does in dozens of contexts. Thirdly, "the Word," as a concept, is elsewhere confined to prologues and does not occur in the body of an argument. See chapter 1 of the Gospel and the Epistle. Fourthly, the tone of the words is alien to the New Testament. This clear-cut analysis of the Trinity has a precision which was not yet known. In the fifth place, it would be difficult to explain how the three divine persons "bear witness" in heaven, for whom the witness would be made, and why. And lastly, the addition of the phrase "and these three are one" does undoubtedly break the sense.

We have discussed this question in detail because devout Christians are sensitive about the methods of textual criticism. They have had cause for complaint, and sometimes for suspicion. Moffatt's quite unjustifiable transpositions of verses and whole paragraphs are an illustration of the irresponsible attitude which scholarship has sometimes revealed towards the text of Scripture. That text must be approached with reverence, without preconceived opinions or private prejudice, and with the sole object of establishing the true reading. That is why we have dropped verse 7 in our rendering.

Verse 6 as translated above, is from the Greek texts on which both the Authorized Version and Revised Version are based. It is to be noted that in two most ancient, the Sinaitic and the Alexandrine, the words "and Spirit" are added after the word "blood." The reference would be to the Baptist's testimony in John 1:32-34. The added phrase would not solve for us the difficulty of the words which precede. Note that John inserts an emphatic repetition, "not through water only, but through water and blood." The statement is perplexing, but if we knew the full nature of the false teaching which John seems anxious to refute, we should be able with greater certainty to interpret it. The best conjecture seems to relate the teaching of the verse to the heresy of Cerinthus. This liberal, if we may risk the term in an ancient setting, distinguished between Jesus and the Christ. The divine Christ, he taught, descended on Jesus at the baptism in Jordan. Christ came "through water," and this may have been a technical term of the heretic theology. Cerinthus went on to teach that the same divine Christ left the human Jesus at the Crucifixion. Thus, He came not "through blood," and the cross and the Incarnation in the process lost their meaning. Redemption, as the New Testament knows it, was excluded. In its place was put the Gnostic's spiritual illumination. The verse is therefore best taken as a firm insistence on the deity of Jesus Christ throughout the entire course of His earthly life, before the baptism and after the Crucifixion.

The water, the symbol of the Lord's consecration to His ministry, and the blood, the symbol of His atoning death, interpreted by the Spirit's testimony, contain the full significance of the gospel. There is something altogether fitting in this clear note of evangelism as the New Testament rounds off its canon. Any, then or now, who deny the truth involved, reject New Testament Christianity.

Note the touch of pathos in verses 8 to 10. John is old, and there were doubtless those who feared the day when the last witness to Christ's earthly presence should pass from them. John, with that quiet urgency which underlies these verses, points out that there is an undying witness greater far than that of man, God Himself whose Spirit indwells the believer's very heart. The one who keeps on believing in the Son of God need not fear if the frail testimony of man is withdrawn. The present participle with the notion of consistent and continuing faith is to be noted. It is through our faith that the Spirit ministers to us. It is interesting to note that John constructs the verb "believe" with the proposition "to." This is his favorite construction in the Gospel. It occurs there forty times as against ten times in the whole of the rest of the New Testament. The metaphor contained in the words is that of faith moving out towards a worthy object. How appropriate that John should close the theme of his last writings (verse 13 to the end are a postscript) with the thoughts that dominate his Gospel.

Note, finally, the subtle analysis of the process by which

the soul finds the assurance of faith. First, a man must believe God. Verse 10 has not the construction with the preposition "to" mentioned above. It simply implies the acceptance of a testimony. The historic witness of the New Testament must be accepted as valid. The next stage is believing in Christ, the self-surrender which is the logical consequence of accepting the wondrous story as true. The last stage is the comfort and confirmation of the inward testimony of God in the heart. As in the picture of Revelation 3:20, we hear the voice, open the door, and He sups with us.

11

AM I A
COMPROMISER?

1 John 5:13-21

"These things I wrote to you that you may know that you have eternal life, you who believe in the name of the Son of God. And, this is the boldness we have towards Him, that if we earnestly ask anything according to His will, He hears us. And if we know that He hears whatever we thus ask, we know that we have whatever we have asked of Him. If anyone sees his brother sinning a sin which is not unto death, he shall ask, and God will give him life, to those, that is, who sin not unto death. There is sin unto death. Not concerning that do I say you should make request. All unrighteousness is sin; and there is sin which is not unto death." 1 John 5:13-17

The letter is finished. It only remains to sum up and conclude. In his eagerness to warn and to instruct, John finds it impossible to recapitulate without introducing new material, so the final verses become a postscript.

The Gospel was written that men might believe in God's incarnate Son (John 20:31), and so have eternal life. The Epistle was added, that those who thus have eternal life may know that they possess it. In chapter 1 (v. 4) the same aim had been expressed in slightly different words. It is the knowledge of the priceless possession which inspires the joy, the blessed assurance of the well-known hymn that "Jesus is mine."

It is a little difficult to trace a connection between verse 13 and verse 14. It is perhaps most logical to assume that verse 14 looks forward rather than backward. We have had occasion to note several times John's fears on the problem of the heretic sects which so endangered God's people. John believed that there were those who so determinedly rejected Christ, that it was useless to pray for them. "There is sin unto death" (v. 16). He is remembering the Lord's words to the Pharisees (Mark 3:22-30), who had similarly confused God and the devil. The Capernaum Pharisees, in the audacity of their hate, ascribed Christ's work to the powers of evil. To misrepresent and corrupt goodness and truth was to demonstrate evil so determined and accepted, a spirit so wilfully lost to good, that such men were already beyond recovery. They were of their father the devil and doing his desires. Dante pictures in his *Inferno* a friar whose soul was in hell while his body walked the earth.

In view of this momentous statement, John recapitulates. For the fourth time he touches on the subject of the Christian's boldness before his God. In 2:28 and 4:17 the context is that of the Judgment Day. In 3:21,22 and here, the reference is to intercessory prayer. It is to be noted in verse 14 that "ask" is what Greek grammar calls a middle verb. Such formations are more intimate and personal than their corresponding actives. The insertion of "earnestly" is an attempt to render this notion. The main theme of the verse is a familiar one, but we may pause for a moment to reconsider it. We are not expected to find out God's will before we pray. We should ever pray with the Gethsemane proviso, "Thy will be done" (Matt. 26:42). We are blessedly safe, since His will is ever for our good. It is the experience of most Christians that God seldom answers our prayers after the shape and fashion of our expectations, or quite in the manner we are so prone to think. The promise is simply that He hears. He answers in His own transcendent way. It is in this sense that "we have whatever we have asked of Him."

In such faith, said John, we should pray for our stumbling brother, unless his sin be "unto death." Even then we are not expressly forbidden to pray. Note the last sentence of verse 16, "Not concerning that do I say you should make request." The last two words translated a humbler less urgent and less suppliant verb than that which is used for "ask" in verses 14, 15 and 16. It is as though the apostle feels that prayer for such desperately wicked sinners must take care to avoid presumption.

Verse 16 does not specify a particular "sin unto death." There is no indefinite article in the Greek text. There is sin which is unto death. It is not an act of sin which is in question, but an attitude towards Christ. What then is involved? The question is of very great importance but cannot be considered outside the whole context of the New Testament. Was not the arch-persecutor of the Church the great Apostle to the Gentiles? Had not Peter denied his Lord with oath and curses? Was not the dying thief accepted in the last agonized hour of an evil life? We know that spiritual ruin comes from one cause alone—rejection of Christ. And experience makes it clear that such rejection can be so constant and consummate that before death closes the day of opportunity a soul may be hardened, ruined, and thrust beyond hope. The persistent and willful choice of darkness instead of light, of the false in place of the true, of the world instead of the Lord, can destroy all power of response. Looking at the self-willed evil of those who made havoc of his Gospel, and at the subtle wickedness of those who perverted the simplicity of his message, the apostle saw sin so calculated and deliberate that he felt prayer for the sinner die on his lips. He could not ask his flock to intercede for those who plotted such cynical ruin for their souls.

Applying his words to our own life and testimony, let us beware of too hasty decision. There are those today for whom it would be idle to pray. In this age of monumental sin there are those for whom the Church at large has raised no supplication. For the many antichrists who still afflict us, it is perhaps useless to intercede. We can but pray that their plans find confusion, and that the judgment of Him who alone judges shall fall upon them. In the narrower circle of our more immediate experience we sometimes find it impossible to frame a prayer for this one or that, especially perhaps in cases of open-eyed apostasy. Nevertheless, have we not also been at times rebuked by the restoration or conversion of one we have too hastily judged to be beyond the pale? It is obvious that the matter is one for which no rules can be drawn up, least of all rules with tabulations of mortal and venial sins. The most solemn warning is one which touches all of us. The starved body becomes less and less able to receive food. And the soul likewise, which stifles all spiritual impulses, can little by little become unable to respond. The malady is one which can afflict the Christian, destroy joy and usefulness, and damage testimony.

The Expositor's Greek Testament, whose commentary on this letter by David Smith is extremely good, illustrates the point by two telling quotations. The first is from Charles Darwin in a letter to a friend dated June 17, 1868. "I am glad you were at the *Messiah*, it is the one thing I should like to hear again, but I dare say I should find my soul too dried up to appreciate it as in old days; and then I should feel very flat, for it is a horrid bore to feel as I constantly do, that I am a withered leaf for every subject except science."

The second quotation is from Richard Baxter, the great

preacher whose statue stands in the busy square of the little Worcestershire town of Kidderminster. A score of miles up the lovely Severn valley is the town of Bridgnorth of which Baxter wrote: "Bridgnorth had made me resolve that I should never go among a people that had been hardened in unprofitableness under an awakening ministry; but either to such as had never had a convincing preacher, or to such as had profited by him." The quotations illustrate that spiritual awareness can die. We are forbidden to judge and should look to our own response to God's Spirit rather than elsewhere. Above all let us beware of usurping a place which is not ours, and of circumscribing the grace and power of God by false limits of our own.

"We know that everyone who has been born of God does not continue in sin, but He who was born of God preserves him, and the Evil One never lays hold of him. We know that we belong to God and that the whole world lies in the power of the Evil One. We know that the Son of God has come and has given us understanding to know the real God. And we are in Him who is real, even in His Son Jesus Christ. This is the real God and life eternal. Little children keep clear of idols."
1 John 5:18-21

"Let us finally," John seems to say, "turn from the dark mysteries of sin, apostasy and perdition, and close with the splendid certainties of the faith which is ours. And let me sum up all I have said to you in three grand assertions." These follow in verses 18, 19, and 20, each introduced by a ringing "we know." The first combines what was said in 3:9 and 2:3; the second contains the essence of 1:6; 2:15,18; 3:10,13; and the third summarizes 4:9-11 and 5:1-12. Together they sum up the central message of the Epistle, that, through the coming of God's Son, we have fellowship with God, and that in that fellowship we have salvation from sin and are set in complete and total opposition to the world.

We have remarked on the nature of the Greek present tense. To translate verse 18, "We know that everyone who is born of God does not sin," is both to contradict fact, to destroy the assurance which this letter sets out to give, and to run counter to other statements of the same writer. The present tense implies continuity, habit, permanence. A child of God may sin and John has recognized the fact as lately as verse 16, but his normal state is detestation of sin and opposition to it. Two things a true Christian never does. He never makes light of sin, and he never admits any sin to be invincible. Hence the translation suggested above.

In the latter half of this verse the rendering of the Authorized Version is unfortunate. In Greek the form of the pronoun "him" differs from that of the pronoun "himself" by one letter only. As may be easily imagined, this is a frequent source of corruption in the text. Some manuscripts here read "him" and some "himself." It becomes certain that "him" is the correct reading when the tense of a participle earlier in the verse is examined. A little more Greek grammar here becomes necessary. Note that whenever John speaks of one "born of God" he uses the perfect participle (3:9; 5:1,4). We have already shown how this participle expresses a state following an event or action. This is an exact rendering of the spiritual situation. A person is born of God by faith, and the blessed state abides. There is assurance in the very tense of the expression. Now in the first half of verse 18 we have the usual form, the perfect participle. Here without doubt, is the Christian. In the second half of the verse, the participle is aorist, and contains the notion of a single act. Here undoubtedly is Christ. Hence the translation given ("who has been born" and "who was born").

How essential it is that Christ should here enter in. There is little comfort in the thought that we should keep ourselves. We know ourselves too well. Harmony is at once secured between Epistle and Gospel. "I was keeping them in Thy name," said the Lord (John 17:12), and three verses later He prays; "I do not ask Thee to take them out of the world, but to keep them from the evil one."

Such salvation belongs to the Christian. The world has no share in it. It is possessed by its Prince and held in a tyranny which knows no relaxation. It follows that the severance which divides a pagan system and the Church of God is as complete as that which sunders God and the Evil One. The verb used in verse 19 is vivid. The phrase runs literally, "lies in the evil one," held in a grim embrace. Those who seek verbal contrasts might turn from this uncompromising statement to Deuteronomy 33:27: "The Eternal God is thy refuge and underneath are the everlasting arms" (*KJV*). In the light of these firm closing statements of the New Testament dare any Christian cherish illusions? The world is the same world, and its Prince and possessor unchanged.

Nevertheless, let no one fear, for "we know that the Son of God has come and given us understanding to know the real God." This is the apostle's last word of assurance to his beloved people, distracted and puzzled by the deviant sects who were perverting the message of the Apostles. It was the true God, the real God, whom the humblest of them found revealed in Christ. The faith was not, as those forerunners of liberal theology maintained, one of many attempts to reach up and touch the infinite. The literature of the ancient world is often eloquent of human questioning to find the real, the true. Christian preaching was quick to see that it had the goal to offer the answer, and not another form of questioning. Such was Paul's theme at Athens; such is the theme of this letter. Christianity is rooted in the concrete and historical. Christ came, and with Him finality. God had no more to say. With this message the first Christians confronted the pagan world. There is no other with which to confront a world as pagan today.

Hence the farewell warning. Do not abandon the real for the illusory. The Greek for idol contains the notion of unreality. Plato uses the word for illusory appearances which stand in contrast to realities. On the other hand, it must be admitted that everywhere in the New Testament idols have concrete significance, and mean precisely the graven images of paganism.

We tend to forget the pervasive nature of the idolatry which moved Paul's spirit in Athens. Every street through which the Christian walked was full of the offense; every heathen house he visited confronted him with the graven image; temples swarmed; the guild feast of his trade organization opened with libation before the statue of the pagan patron deity; his meat troubled his conscience in case it should be part of beasts sacrificed to idols; the Emperor's statue stood as the symbol of man in the place of God, and many a Christian had died and was to die for his refusal to place one pinch of incense in the brazier at its feet. If such abomination was more apparent in one ancient city than another, that city was Ephesus. The very economic life of the city was centered in the worship of Artemis whose image, doubtless a meteoric stone, had fallen from heaven. Ephesian coins may be seen in any museum, stamped with idolatrous figures. The Christian had to handle them. Ephesian tokens and charms were a major export of the great heathen port.

It is clear from New Testament history that John had spent much of his ministry in combat with compromising elements in the Church who saw no reason why the Christian should not, to some measure, come to terms with the pervasive paganism around him. Those flayed in the uncompromising language of Jude and Second Peter, those castigated in Revelation as the followers of Balaam and Jezebel, and the Nicolaitans, are the group who had once endangered and were still endangering the healthy life of the Church. John feared the human weakness of those to whom he wrote. It was not that he expected them to take part in idolatrous rites, though such an attitude meant abstention from every social and civic function. What he more greatly feared was that the sheer pressure of the enveloping pagan society would encourage ways of accommodation and result in damaging compromise. It is also possible that the Nicolaitan attitude had been taken up by the Gnostic cults. We have no clear evidence that such was their teaching, but we have had occasion to note some of the perilous doctrines they taught. It is surely unlikely that many among them would have regarded their gospel as worth dying for, or as worth too large a measure of uncomfortable ostracism in the pagan world.

If John had in mind literal idols, the fact may be conceded that there are other idols than those which are constructed of wood and stone. John would no doubt agree with the host of Christian preachers of all centuries who have variously applied his words to a thousand substitutes for God. He no doubt saw in the idols of his Ephesian streets the sign and symbol of the false, the evil, and the base, the exaltation of man, and that usurpation of the place of God which is the root and inspiration of idolatry the world over.

The last apostle's last words there find their modern application. There are still substitutes for God, be they embedded in political ideas, social systems, sub-Christian cults. It matters what we believe. Such is the insistent note of this Epistle. God is still found revealed in Christ. In a world still pagan, still subtly cursed with idolatries, salvation is still found in committal of the life to Him who forgives, saves, keeps.

SECOND JOHN

12
AM I
TRUE?
2 John 1-13

"The elder, to Kuria, his fellow-Christian, and her children—whom I love in truth, and not I only, but all who have come to a knowledge of the truth, because of the truth that dwells in us and shall be with us for ever. Yes, there shall be with us grace, mercy and peace from God the Father and the Lord Jesus Christ, the Father's Son, in truth and love." 2 John 1-3

The question of "the elect Lady" has been answered, tentatively, above. John begins formally in the third person, but passes rapidly to the more intimate first. The recurrent references to truth were not uncolored by the famous words of Christ, "I am the Way, the Truth and the Light." It was a rich truth which they held, no mere philosophy or code. It was a reality as personal as the Lord, dominating thought, words, action. It was a purifying love in the midst of a corrupt environment where love was the damaged casualty of the times, as it is today.

"I am overjoyed because I have found some of your young people walking in truth, according to the commandment we received from the Father." 2 John 4

There is a story of John's riding out into the hills behind Smyrna to find and to win back a young man who had joined a gang of thieves. The old man loved young people, and was glad to see them carrying on the truth, an uncorrupted gospel, into the next century. These young people were evidently the nephews (and nieces perhaps) of the lady addressed. In Ephesus, the pagan home of Artemis, the sex-ridden den of superstition and evil, these

115

young folk had learned to walk a clean courageous way. Of such is the future of man, if future there be. In Christ is no "generation gap," as Paul and Timothy had shown in Paul's last letter a generation earlier. And that letter (2 Timothy) is light on the tension and temptation of living at Ephesus as a Christian.

"And now I ask you Kuria, not as if I were writing you a commandment which you did not know, but one which we have had from the beginning—that we love one another. And this is the love I mean, that we live as he commanded us. This is the commandment, just as you heard from the beginning—that you live in it." 2 John 5,6

We have rendered the common metaphor "walk" in both verses by live. "To walk in truth" and "to walk in love" are identical. Love is true living. To love is to be true. The thought has returned to John's insistence in the first letter. He is remembering the conversation which haunted him (John 13:34,35), and that has led him to an adjacent memory (John 14:15).

"I stress this because many deceivers have gone out into the world who do not agree that Jesus was the Messiah, coming in the flesh. This is what I mean by deceiver and antichrist. Look to yourselves that we do not destroy what we have wrought but receive our full wages. The 'progressive' who does not remain in the teaching of Christ has not God. The one who remains in the teaching of Christ, he has both the Father and the Son." 2 John 7-9

116

Without an undiminished Christ there is no Christianity. A Jesus any less than God in flesh appearing cannot be a Saviour. Any doctrine which takes away from Christ's full deity is no doctrine at all. It is antichristian, destructive, ruinous. But seducers, deceivers were at work. That is why John wrote his first letter and his Gospel. In 1 John 4:2, the tense was different. There it was "come" or "has come" in the flesh, as though to stress the historic fact of the Incarnation. Now he uses a present, "coming," as though that act, like Calvary, was somehow timeless. Jesus is always the Messiah. We always, day by day, look to him to see God.

In verse 8 John seems to be addressing the whole congregation. It is most likely that he expected the vital part of his letter to be read to the Christian community. We want, he says, to receive all that the faith for which we have striven can give us—no attenuated reward, no docked wage—but the whole.

The word at the beginning of verse 9, which we have rendered in quotes was a term used by the deviant sects. They were "advanced thinkers," "progressives." It has been the favorite device of all such wreckers to claim that they abandon no truth, only make it conform to the times. John was no static thinker. His Gospel was to weave into the New Testament rich areas of new truth. On the other hand, he did not abandon anything that was revealed. Any new statement of truth must contain all that which has been revealed as true. It must "remain in the teaching of Christ." There is no special gospel for any century, no theology for any particular land. There are aspects of the gospel which apply more relevantly here than there in contexts geographical and historical. But let every man beware as he seeks to express

117

the gospel of Christ to his contemporaries or to those in some other culture, not to diminish revealed truth or to change the face of Christ in the process. The "teaching of Christ" is the teaching which stresses the fact that Christ was God's revelation of Himself, the full and final message to man. Any other version of Christ, any distortion of the record, loses not only the Christ John had known but loses God too. Christ was the way to the Father. Lose one and the other is lost. Such warning is timeless.

"If anyone comes to you and does not bring with him this teaching, do not receive him into your home, do not even greet him, for the one who greets him shares his evil deeds." 2 John 10,11

These are drastic words and seem both to contradict John's own reiterated insistence on the primacy of love, and the common insistence of the New Testament on the duty of hospitality. Several facts, however, of the historical situation must be remembered. First, the homes of the Christians were their places of assembly and worship. To receive a dangerous heretic into the home was to expose a whole Christian group to his false teachings and to give his perilous message a platform. Secondly, these were dangerous days. The faith was abroad in a world permeated by Greek thought and the speculative spirit which arose from it. To waver at this time concerning Christian truth, to shake the foundations so painfully laid, would be to lose all. Christianity would have evolved into one of the barren philosophies of which the world was full. The last eye-witness felt the burden of his enormous responsibility. He could die happy if he saw the truth, for which he had suffered, established and safe. Hence the uncommon vehemence against the designing men who were infiltrating the Church, preying on its members, and damaging the souls of men. See it all in context and the old writer's urgency and firmness are easily understood. John could be nothing less than clear and strong. "Do not say good day, do not say goodbye" (both welcome and farewell are contained in the word). Such saboteurs were not welcome. Freeze them out of Asia, was his direction.

"Though I have many matters to write to you about, I have decided not to do so with ink and paper. But I hope to visit you and speak face to face, that our joy may be complete. The children of your Christian sister greet you." 2 John 12,13

Many sheets of papyrus, averaging eight by ten inches have been found. On such a sheet John or his helper wrote. Papyrus was an immensely more convenient writing material than the Babylonian clay tablet. But with a reed pen and ink made of glue and soot one did not write with the facility of good paper and a ball-point pen. It was encouragement to be brief, not always a bad policy.

Besides, there was counsel to give in the menacing situation already hinted at, which John thought it best not to put on paper. Many have lived to regret words given permanence in writing, words which have returned to lash or to convict the writer. It is always good to think twice before committing thought to paper. It might have been easier to write hard words in Ephesus than to say them in Smyrna or Hierapolis, or wherever the letter went. John knew from experience that the words said were easier to recall. There was opportunity for constructive reply, for more rapid interchange and explanation and for the softening of personal intercourse.

It seems from the limitation of greetings to the children that the sister in Ephesus was no longer living. So ends a small human document, a gentle and gracious message of a famous man, revealing his loving but steadfast personality, casting a gleam of light into a little church. We would not be without it.

THIRD JOHN

13
SHALOM
3 John 1:15

"The Elder to Gaius, the beloved, whom I love in truth. Dear man, in everything I pray that you may prosper and be in health, just as your soul prospers, for I am very glad that brethren keep coming and testifying to the truth you hold and the truth you live by. I have no greater gladness than hearing that my children live by the truth." 3 John 1-4

Gaius had stood the test. Perhaps there is significance in John's promise of prayer for his friend's prosperity and health. The hostility of Diotrephes may have been a menace to both. A menace met with steadfastness and Christian grace. Health is a matter of mind and spirit as well as of the body. David Smith, in his commentary in *"The Expositor's Greek Testament,"* quotes quaintly William Law, whose *Serious Call to a Devout and Holy Life* was published in 1728. It is perhaps the most influential book after *Pilgrim's Progress* to be published since the Reformation. "Flavia," he writes, "would be a miracle of piety if she was but half as careful of her soul as she is of her body. The rising of a pimple on her face, the sting of a gnat, will make her keep her room for two or three days, and she thinks they are very rash people that do not take care of things in time." William Penn wrote similarly in 1692, in his *Fruits of Solitude:* "He is curious to wash, dress and perfume his body, but careless of his soul. The one shall have many hours, the other not so many minutes."

Health in the realms of thought and emotion, in mind and soul, is a prerequisite, as modern medicine would agree, for all health of body. And such well-being does not come without attention.

"Dear man, it is a work of faith you are doing, whenever you render service to the brethren and strangers. They have told the church of your love, and you will do well to send them on their way worthily of God, for they came for the sake of the Name, taking nothing from pagans. It is therefore our duty to entertain such people that we may become fellow-workers for the truth."
3 John 5-8

James would have approved of the opening remark. Literally, the words read, "You do a thing of faith." Faith and works blessedly commingle. "You will do well" or "You do well" is a phrase found in the papyri for "Please." We might say, "Please always send them on as God would have you do." A papyrus from Oxyrhynchus contains a note, "I sent you the bread-basket by the camel driver Taurinos. Please let me know that you received it." The Greek runs as it does in verse 6, "You will do well . . ." To send a person on his way was a courtesy accorded an important or respected visitor and involved escorting him over the first part of the journey. (See Acts 15:3 and Titus 3:13.) Homer, in *Odyssey* 15:74, says: "Welcome the coming, speed the parting guest."

"I wrote somewhat to the church but Diotrephes, who likes to hold first place among them, does not accept me. That is why, if I come, I shall call his conduct into question for he is slandering me with evil words. And not content with that, neither does he himself accept the brethren but also prevents those who wish to and puts them out of the church." 3 John 9,10

Dr. A. Plummer, who produced his fine commentary on John's letters for *The Cambridge Greek Testament* in 1886, remarks: "That any Christian should be found to act in this manner towards the last surviving apostle is nothing less than astounding." Living in that brief noontide of episcopal authority, Dr. Plummer overlooked the audacity of evil. Nor is it likely that Diotrephes could be counted a Christian. A dozen verses from John's first letter could be quoted to strip such a title from him. Strange birds nest in the mustard tree, and the breed who find in the Christian congregation a stage for their personal ambitions or a sphere of arrogance and personal aggrandizement, have not been confined to any one time or place. Like the poor, those who wish to be first are always with us.

John's letter, introducing and commending a Christian mission party, had not checked the conduct of the trouble maker of the congregation in question. He was evidently powerful enough to prevent their acceptance by the well-disposed. Diotrephes, probably being a slanderer, gossip, tattler (all three words could render the verb of verse 10), no doubt invoked the rules that were taking shape on hospitality. The Didache, an early Christian manual of Christian morals and Church practice, lays down some firm guidelines to guard against "Christ-traffickers," people who made personal profit out of religion. One rule runs: "The apostle is not to remain for more than one day, or, if need be, two. If he remains three, he is a false prophet. And when he departs, he is to take nothing but food to last him until his next lodging for the night. If he asks for money he is a false prophet." These were the ancestors of the begging friars who lived on the kindness of the Church and of the alleged pilgrims to the Holy Land (la Sainte Terre) who put the word "saunterer" into English.

Care was necessary and it could temper hospitality. In the Didache there are detailed directions given by which to judge the genuineness of the itinerant or visiting preacher. They still apply. The fault with the rebel Diotrephes was that he was using valid rules against the guarantee and recommendation of a revered leader of the Church.

"If I come," says the old man. It was yet another burden on his years and he did not know whether he could carry it so far.

"Dear man, do not imitate evil. Imitate good. The one who does good is of God. The one who does evil has not seen God. Demetrius has everyone's recommendation and that of the truth itself. We recommend him and you know that our recommendation is true. I had much to write about to you but I do not want to write with ink and pen. I hope soon to see you, and we shall speak face to face. Peace be yours. Your friends greet you. Greet my friends by name." 3 John 11-15

There was a Demetrius (Demas is the shortened form as Silas for Silvanos) in the churches of the Lycus Valley thirty years before (Col. 4:14, Philem. 24). A Demas disappointed Paul in A.D. 67 (2 Tim. 4:10). There is no reason to suppose that John is speaking of the same man, now perhaps in later middle age. Much less can we identify this fine person with the Demetrius who, in the same Ephesus (Acts 19:24), once made silver shrines for the pilgrims to the temple of Artemis. Anyone so minded could write a historical novel on such an identification, a story of dramatic conversion, running well, backsliding and restoration—but fiction it would need to be.

The letter ends like its predecessor. John was, it seems, planning a circuit tour. And so he passes from history. "Peace be yours." It is the old Hebrew, the modern Israeli salutation, *Shalom.* It comes echoing down the long corridor of time to us, *Shalom, shalom. . . .*